MORMON WOMEN

MORMON WOMEN

Portraits & Conversations

James N. Kimball

and

Kent Miles

Handcart Books | Salt Lake City

Mormon Women: Portraits & Conversations
Copyright ©2009 James N. Kimball and Kent Miles.
All rights reserved. Published by Handcart Books,
a division of White Horse Books. No portion of this
book may be reproduced in any form without the express
written permission of the publisher, Handcart Books.
Printed in the United States.

Photos: Kent Miles
Cover design: Pat Bagley
Editors: Dan F. Thomas and Elbert Peck

First Edition
9   8   7   6   5   4   3   2   1

ISBN 978-0-9801406-1-3

Handcart Books
1347 S. Glenmare St.
Salt Lake City, Utah 84105
801-556-4615
www.handcartbooks.com

in memory of
Jim Kimball

Contents

Preface

Jim Kimball and I were friends for thirty years when we began work on this book. For a long time we had wanted to do a project together, but nothing ever got off the ground. One day my father made a suggestion: "Why not tell the story of Mormon women? They're really key to the success of the LDS Church, but their story never gets told." Right away, Jim and I knew we had found our project.

There was just one problem: we happened to be two Mormon *men*. What made us think that a book about women should be put together by a couple of guys? Shouldn't it be a women's project? Does anybody really need more men talking on behalf of women?

We decided that our role would be as documentarians. We would base the project on something done too rarely: women conversing about women's lives. We would get them talking, and we would listen.

We both wanted to focus on women who inspired us, who were doing their best to live the gospel while negotiating the deep waters of modern-day life. We were interested in women notable for their own accomplishments, rather than who they were married to. Women of high position in the Church already had plenty of official visibility. We wanted to dispel the stereotypes about Mormon women, held by some and reinforced by popular media. We wanted to interview women of courage, valor and compassion. In retrospect, we were looking for women not unlike our own mothers and wives, sisters and daughters.

Where to begin? Like good returned missionaries, we started with friends and asked them for referrals. There was no shortage. Everyone knew a woman who should be included. We started with people in and around Utah. Soon we were in Los Angeles, then the East Coast. Eventually, we would find our way to Russia, Ukraine, South Africa, Brazil, Argentina, Japan, Hong Kong, the Philippines and Australia.

We spent years traveling the globe, eventually interviewing more than thirty women. The project gave us wonderful and surprising experiences. I remember visiting Dornach, Scotland, where we met with Anne Perry. At church, she was just one of the branch members, just "Sister Perry." There was no sense that fame and fortune had separated her from the rest of the congregation.

I remember being overwhelmed by the matter-of-fact way Maria "Chelito" Dimaya told of being captured and tortured by the Filipino military. She bore her testimony to me that the Mormon Church had more power to instigate social change than all the guns and all the revolutionaries in the world, because the gospel of Christ changed the hearts and desires of people. As we concluded our interview, she told me she was going to look for a new place to live. A typhoon the previous week had flooded her family out, yet she still had taken the time for our interview.

I remember Tsobinar Tadevosyan talking about her imprisonment in the Soviet Gulag and how the experience had been a great blessing to her. Everyone there had been prisoners of conscience—artists, writers, intellectuals, the shining lights of her generation—and she was grateful to be included among them.

Everywhere we traveled, each interview was a gift. Jim and I thought these women had stories everyone would benefit from hearing. They each display the courage to allow their natural abilities and interests to find expression in their lives. They each make the best effort to live according to gospel standards, but they are not perfect. They make sacrifices, finding their way as they go, making compromises between the demands of life when they need to. But they do not allow themselves to become enslaved by external expectations. They roll with life's punches. When they're knocked down, they get up, dust themselves off, adapt to the lessons learned, and go on to do what is in them to do.

These are ordinary LDS women. And that is what this book celebrates.

In late 2003, Jim was diagnosed with an inoperable brain tumor. He passed away the next spring. He made it clear that he wanted our project finished and published, but it was difficult to carry on without the spark of his irresistible humor. *Mormon Women* was put on the back burner, but never forgotten.

In late 2007, I got a call from Cambria Judd and Michelle Williams—they are neighbors of Jim's son, Ted. They had gotten ahold of the manuscript and were determined to see the project finished. We all met to evaluate the existing material. Our fears were that it might have become dated with the passing of a decade. In reality, the interviews seemed to increase in relevance and timeliness. The women we spoke with had tapped into a wellspring of wisdom and human experience.

Ted's desire to honor his father's legacy, combined with Cami pushing and Michelle pulling, made it possible for us to bring this book to life. With the help of the good people at Handcart Books, we came up with a plan to publish a first volume that would include fourteen of the interviews we conducted, along with portraits I took at the time of each interview.

There are still many stories to tell.

Kent Miles
Salt Lake City, Utah
July 2008

Foreword

A book like this is long overdue, and so it is a great honor for me to write the foreword to *Mormon Women: Portraits & Conversations*. This book recognizes the impact women can have in all aspects of our rapidly changing world, celebrating the insight, courage and determination these women bring to their lives. I feel especially privileged because two of these women, Emma Lou Thayne and Christine Durham, are close friends, mentors and role models who have had a lasting impact on my life.

Governor Olene Walker

These are stories of hope and inspiration. There is a common thread of service and faith, as these fourteen women have excelled in their respective realms. Each of their journeys is unique, illustrating what one ordinary person can accomplish when they put their trust in the Lord. What great examples and guideposts they are for women everywhere who have the desire to reach out and make the world a better place.

I met Emma Lou Thayne in college, and I have many fond memories of time spent with her during those years. Soon I became aware of her amazing academic abilities. Over the years we have remained close, and when it came time to refine my inaugural speech, I immediately thought of her magical use of words. Christine Durham is a person for whom I have always had the greatest respect and admiration. She is a woman of tremendous insight and wisdom, and I relied on her expertise while I served in the legislative and executive branches for the State of Utah. Indeed it was a highlight for me when Chief Justice Durham (a woman) swore me in as fifteenth governor of Utah (a woman).

I was touched as I read about the heroism of Carol Gray, leading convoys into war-torn Bosnia; how she knew that "when the Lord is on your side, when you have a desire to help, he gives you the ability to do it." This is a wish I have for all women—to reach inside themselves, discover their inner potential, and put that knowledge to good use. Every woman is a daughter of God, capable of accomplishing tasks that only *seem* insurmountable.

I was equally impressed when I read the story of Cecile Pelous helping orphans in India and Nepal. She exemplifies what can happen when one has the desire to serve and wholeheartedly embraces a worthwhile cause. Cecile states, "Serving them, I discover in myself talent and energy that I never would have sought for myself. I have been able to do much more than I thought possible, without previous training, but with the sincere desire to serve."

This book gives the reader an opportunity to get to know these women, their families, and share in their life experiences. Scattered around the globe, they all have different stories to tell, but they all discovered that every individual has the ability not only to serve God, but to serve their fellow people. No matter the setting, be it a prison in Siberia, the fashion world of Paris, or the academic world of Harvard, women, Mormon or otherwise, have the capacity to make meaningful and lasting changes.

It is my hope that in reading these stories, women everywhere will be inspired to know that they have the potential within themselves to accomplish the desires of their hearts. And one important lesson that I have learned along the way is that you have to find balance in your life, the balance that works best for you and not anyone else. The women in this book have made great achievements, but each one of them had to balance her professional life with the needs of her family and her church. When we find that balance in our lives, when we work hard and look to our Heavenly Father for strength, I am convinced that we can achieve more than we ever dreamed possible.

Governor Olene Walker
St. George, Utah
January 2009

MORMON WOMEN

CAROL GRAY is a British homemaker who became a recognized humanitarian leader in Europe and Africa. She began by organizing relief aid for victims of the Balkan War. Four years later, she had personally delivered over two dozen truck convoys of food, clothing, and medical supplies to Bosnia. She went on to found Hugs International, TLC, which operates an orphanage, school, and medical center in Ghana.

Carol Gray

Humanitarian
Sheffield, England

My parents joined the LDS Church when I was about five. It's challenging to be a member of the Church in England. We don't have the privileges they have in Utah, where there's an LDS chapel on every corner. We have to work hard for everything, but I wouldn't have it any other way. It's wonderful. And I'm the sort of person that when my back's against the wall and I've got a challenge, that's when I fight my hardest.

I married my husband, Stuart, when I was twenty-one. He has a property business in Sheffield, England, where we live. Our home is always full. We've got people in and out all the time. I have seven children, three grandsons, and lots of adopted kids who come and live with us. We take them in and get them married off.

When I had my patriarchal blessing,[1] it told me that my life would be spared for a special purpose. I never gave that much thought until I was twenty-eight and was diagnosed with terminal cancer. The doctors rushed me into the hospital and performed an emergency operation. They stitched me up and told my husband that I had about three months to live, at the most.

I didn't know this until later, but as I was being wheeled out, we passed by a world-renowned surgeon who was visiting the hospital. He inquired what was wrong with me. They told him, "She's dying. There's nothing we can do for her. The cancer is too extensive, so we've shut her back up and we're sending her home to spend her remaining time with her family." But he said, "She's only a young woman. She's too young to die." I had four girls then, and my youngest daughter was six months old.

He performed an experimental operation on me, which had only been done twice before. One gentleman died in the operating theatre and another lady died ten days after surgery, so I'm the only survivor of this operation. They did all sorts of things. It's not my first wish to go into it, but I'm basically a mass of plastic tubing and steel bars inside, and I live virtually on tablets. Every day I take a pound of pills that keep my body going because I'm minus most of the things that regulate the normal functioning of the body.

With the fasting and prayers of members in my stake,[2] I knew that my patriarchal blessing had come to pass. I'd obviously been saved for something.

---

1. A personal blessing that provides the recipient spiritual counsel and guidance. It is transcribed and individuals refer to it throughout their life.

2. A group of LDS congregations, similar to a diocese.

Five years later I had three little boys, which I was told I should never have had. My body wasn't geared up for having children, so when I delivered our first miracle son, Jamie, it was incredible. Then we had twin boys two-and-a-half years later. Their births hit all the newspapers around the world because no one could understand how I'd actually had them. I assumed that was the reason why my patriarchal blessing said what it did.

~

I'm a typical Latter-day Saint mom. I've never needed to work and I've always stayed at home with my kids, quite content looking after the family and doing all the loads of artsy-crafty things that Mormon mums tend to do. I enjoy painting, writing poetry, and I love doing flower arrangements. I was always perfectly happy at home and never went far afield, and I've always tried to live my life close to my Savior.

I think you have to be faced with losing your life, not knowing how long you've got on earth, to put your life in order. When you think that maybe you've got only three months left, you forget about getting cross with people or putting things off. You learn to pack so much into every minute. I am grateful to my Heavenly Father for the extra time he has allowed me.

One day a local hospice phoned me. Because of my experience, they asked me if I would volunteer to do bereavement counseling for families who were preparing to lose loved ones. I jumped at the chance.

I got to know some lovely families, but there was one couple in particular who I became very close with. They were old—they must have been in their late eighties—and she was dying with bowel cancer. He was so distraught to see her virtually disappearing before his eyes and being helpless to do anything for her. I spent a lot of time with them. They had no family, so they were all and all to each other.

One day while I was working in the garden, I got a phone call, and it was him. He said, "Carol"—I could tell over the phone how tearful he was— "Carol, can you come to the hospital please? She's going to die." I threw my clothes on, pushed the kids off to the neighbors, and got in the car.

As I started down the driveway, I had this really strong feeling inside that I needed to stop the car and pick a single rose. I just brushed it aside and said, *Don't be silly. The woman is dying. There's no need for you to take her any flowers.* And so I carried on down the drive. But again, this feeling came, this time even more strongly: *Pick a single rose and take it to the hospital.* Again I just pushed it to the side. They needed me there. She was dying.

As I drove out onto the road, I knew in no uncertain terms that something unusual was happening. I pulled the car over, and that feeling reverberated right through every part of my body. It just said—and this time it was very specific—*Turn the car around and go back and pick a single yellow rose.*

And of course, I knew I had been chastised by the Spirit. So I turned the car around, and all the time I'm thinking, *I don't have any yellow roses in my garden. I have pink and red and white and peach and every color you could imagine, but no yellow roses.* It was the only color I didn't have. I pulled the car up to the garden, and facing me on one of my pink rose bushes was the most beautiful yellow rose. It wasn't pure yellow. It was fringed with sissy-pink bits all around the edge, but nevertheless, it was yellow. I just stared at this rose in total disbelief, because in the eight years that I had lived there, that plant had never produced a yellow rose, and I knew every plant in my garden.

I rushed to the hospital, still not knowing what this rose was for. The curtains were pulled around the old lady. She was obviously close to dying. I noticed that he had a hold of her hand, but his head had fallen onto her bed and he just sat there with his head buried. It was a tender moment and I didn't want to intrude, so I just laid the rose by her side and tiptoed out.

He came shuffling down the corridor after me, and he had tears streaming down his eyes. I'll never forget: he shouted my name, I turned 'round and he said, "Carol, how did you know? How did you know today was our wedding anniversary?" Every year on their anniversary, he had given her a single yellow rose. I had no idea, absolutely no idea whatsoever. He had never mentioned that before. But it made me realize that the Lord listens to the hearts of us all, and he had obviously listened to the heart of the old man who was so distressed about losing his life-long companion. And that was their seventieth wedding anniversary.

~

The feeling that prompted me, I know it has prompted me many times in my life. Because of that experience, I was aware of it and I recognized it when it came again. It was that same feeling that came one day when I was watching the Balkan War on the news. We were watching the awful things happening there day after day, night after night, and although I didn't want to see it I was compelled to put it on every day to see how things were going off.

One particular night I was watching a program on all these women who had been released from the Serbian camps. I saw the looks on their faces and I felt this same feeling. I needed to do something, but I didn't know what. I questioned my feelings. I'm not an adventurous woman at all—I wouldn't even go down to the temple in Surrey without my husband. But I felt strongly that the Lord was requesting me to do something more than just take out my checkbook and write a check for a charity.

I spent three or four days on my knees—not all the time obviously, but a lot of time on my knees—pleading with the Lord to help me know what he wanted me to do. I rang up several charities that worked in Bosnia. I asked them, if I started collecting donated items, what would be helpful, and would they take it on their convoy? My intentions were never, ever to go into a war zone. I'm no kamikaze. I love my family far too much to even remotely get involved in anything like that.

It was just before Christmas of 1992, and I went and saw my bishop and proposed that the Relief Society[3] sisters get involved in some compassionate service outside of our area. Within three weeks we had collected thirty-eight tons of aid. We worked day and night boxing and packing all the stuff. People who would never walk into an LDS chapel came in and stood side by side with the Latter-day Saints—sang with them and laughed with them as

---

3. The principal women's organization in the LDS Church, founded in 1842.

they boxed and packed. It was just unbelievable. With it being near Christmas, everyone was infused with a spirit of giving.

As a matter of fact, the whole community became involved—not only our own church, but many other denominations, hospitals, schools, the police force, the GPO (our FedEx). Day after day, wagons kept pulling up and dropping off tents, cooking equipment, emergency medical supplies. It was incredible.

Somebody told the newspapers and they ran stories like "Christmas Carol Bags for Bosnia," "Mother of Seven Bags for Bosnia," and "The Latter-day Saints are Bagging for Bosnia." It really captured people's imagination. Even the BBC picked up the story. That was wonderful because it brought in so much more stuff, but it put me in a tight spot.

I'd already arranged with a local transport company to deliver the cargo to London, where a charity was going to take it off our hands. Two days before, the charity rang me up and said that they were sorry, but they couldn't take it. They'd run out of money and they weren't transporting aid any more. That left me in a real dilemma. Our ward meethinghouse was absolutely cram-packed full. Even the bishop's office was full of baby milk and disposable baby nappies.

That Saturday night a lorry came and dumped twenty tons of aid in front of the chapel doors. On Sunday morning we couldn't get near the chapel, so service wasn't held that day. We spent virtually all of that Sunday moving boxes so people could get into church. I'll tell you, I wasn't the flavor of the month with the bishop.

So now we had all this aid and no way to get it to Bosnia. I was absolutely devastated. I can remember going into the ladies restroom and getting down on my knees and praying to Heavenly Father, *Lord, what have I done? Was I listening to the wrong promptings? Everything's gone wrong. And yet there is all this wonderful stuff that is waiting to go, and they're waiting for it. But I have no means of getting it there.* And more vans and cars were showing up all the time with more donations. It was awful.

There was this one article in the paper that my husband, Stuart, noticed. It said, "Convoy of Hope Bound for Bosnia. Anyone wishing to join this convoy should ring this number." It was a group of people who had collected all their own stuff and they were joining into a convoy. I rang them up, hoping they would be able to take our cargo. They wouldn't. Instead, they said, "We would love to have you join us."

When you voluntarily go into a war zone, all insurance is null and void. Because I've had cancer, and to this day nobody can understand why I'm still walking around, no insurance company will come near me. My husband was going to be the one joining the convoy, but then he would have lost his insurance coverage. I told him, "If you stand on a land mine or if you're shot by a sniper or a shell lands on you, we'll be in a mess. I just have this feeling inside that the Lord wants me to go."

I couldn't explain it, but I knew I would be all right. Stuart wasn't too happy about it, but after a day or so of fasting and praying we came to the conclusion that it would be the best solution. One of my daughters, Samantha, decided that she would come along and drive the truck with me.

She's not a bit like me; she's very adventurous. It was a big, seven-ton truck, which was about twenty-eight feet long—it was a massive thing.

I phoned a lot of friends, both inside and outside the Church, who had big vans and trucks, and many of them came and joined my convoy. There were one hundred and ten vehicles on that first, humongous convoy. It took ten days of driving; two-and-a-half thousand miles. We slept roughly, in minus temperatures, and it was just wonderful.

My stomach was in a knot the whole trip, wondering what I was going to see. It was a massive adventure for me because the only pictures that I'd ever seen of Bosnia were the ones of people blowing each other's brains out. I'm a rather compassionate person at the best of times, and I get very involved with people. I was getting nervous as to how I would react, seeing people in distress, because I don't cope with that very well.

We arrived in the Croatian capital, Zagreb, and there was a large meeting held. There were four hundred drivers altogether. We were asked if any of us would volunteer for the crisis area. I suppose it was because I was naive, having grown up in the Church, and my daughter as well. We both looked at each other and thought, *We've not driven all this way to stick this stuff in some warehouse. We're off to the crisis area to give it to the people.*

But what we didn't realize was that it was a crisis area because it was under shellfire, and no one else was batty enough to go. I can still remember the sinking feeling when Samantha and I looked around and only two other men raised their hands. I knew I had boobed, but I was too proud to renege on the decision. My daughter was so excited, and I wasn't going to let her see that I'm a chicken. So that was how I got into doing these convoys—on false pretenses, really.

I think the Lord did this in the only way he could get me to do it. There was simply no way I was brave enough to have made the decision straight away. I just wasn't that sort of a woman. It was one step at a time, which is the way he always does everything with me.

⁓

That first experience was unbelievable. We went into an area where the Canadian peacekeeping forces were, in a place called Poljana. We had to transfer all those supplies into the back of a huge Bosnian army wagon so the enemy wouldn't know there were civilians. We went through minefields. I don't know whether you've ever been through a minefield or not, but it was quite an experience.

We had to go over a pontoon bridge, which absolutely scared my socks off. I couldn't swim. It was winter and the river was badly swollen. It was only a temporary pontoon bridge, thick beams of wood chained to floating oil drums. Water was already lapping up between the slats and, of course, we had to drive this huge truck over it.

The unfortunate thing was, I hadn't brought my glasses. Although I was fine driving through Europe, I didn't fancy driving across this pontoon bridge. My daughter is an excellent driver, much better than I, so I had her drive. I stood in front and directed her over the bridge, inch by inch. There must have only been a couple of extra inches on either side of the wheels. What I hadn't anticipated was that as the vehicle went onto the bridge, it sunk it down. So there I am—and it sounds crazy, but I always wear skirts, even on convoy—and I'm lifting my skirt higher and higher up my legs because the water was just swishing 'round. It's unnerving when you can't actually see what you're walking on. The water was murky and muddy and very cold. Did I mention that I'm terrified of water?

I immediately recognized that I needed help from Heavenly Father. My legs were stiff and wouldn't move. I was petrified, and I prayed, *Somehow, Lord, you are going to have to work a miracle on my legs and get them moving because I cannot move them myself.*

Immediately after I'd said that, all the fear left. It was unbelievable. The fear was just gone and I was able to walk across with that vehicle. I still don't know how we ever made it. The planks went under the water and so did the chains, which were a guideline as to where the edge of the bridge was. We had an army colonel with us and there were beads of perspiration on his forehead; he was just terrified. My daughter drove that truck without ever looking to the side. She just steered it straight and we made it across.

We went through an area where almost four hundred people had just been killed. It changed me completely. What distressed me more than any-thing was seeing the people. Nothing could have prepared me for their sunken, hollow, lonely eyes. On our journey back, I realized that somehow the Lord had gotten me into something that I couldn't turn away from. That first trip really sealed a love for the people in my heart, which I've never been able to shake off.

A month later, I organized another convoy, and the month after that another one, and that's how it went. The Lord has opened his doors to me and allowed me to go into areas that even the United Nations didn't go in the early days. We'd tell U.N. officials where we'd been and they'd ask how we got there. I'd say, "The villagers took us 'round the back way where they knew I'd be safe." They would respond, "We can't even get in there and we're a peacekeeping force."

Before I went on that first trip, I had a strong feeling that I would be kept safe, that the Lord would look after me. And somehow I knew it had to be me to go. I realize the answer now. In the early days of the war it had to be a woman because a woman wasn't seen as a threat. And the people there were wonderful with me. Whether it was the Bosnians or the Croats or the Serbs, they looked after me so wonderfully well. They are all special people.

One thing you notice is the reason why each person gets involved. You get some people who enjoy the publicity for a moment or two, and some who are in it for other reasons. But on the whole, most people go because they genuinely care.

I remember Mike, a bloke we took on a convoy. You know the SAS, the crack special forces of the British Army? Mike was an ex-SAS paratrooper, very macho, and a born-again Christian. He rang me up, asking to join our next convoy. But he added, "I don't want any of this lovey-dovey stuff. I've heard that your convoys are all a bit lovey-dovey and you put your arms around everybody and tell them that you care. That isn't my scene at all. I just want to go and take the stuff and hand it to them." I said, "Fine, that's lovely."

And all the time we were driving in the convoy, he said, "You're not going to get me putting my arms around nobody. It's not my way."

When we got to the first village, all these old ladies came running out because they recognized our vans. And of course, all the other convoy members were hugging them and there were tears all around. Mike was huffing and puffing, and this dear old lady went up to him and just threw her arms around him. He turned around and tears were streaming down his face. After that, he hugged everything that in a skirt that moved. He was just amazing. He came on several more convoys and he just loved it.

I've been on twenty-three convoys, and over the years the British people, especially the Latter-day Saints, have been wonderful. And my husband, bless his little cotton socks, has put his hand in his pocket so many times to underwrite a convoy. It costs us approximately eight thousand to ten thousand pounds just to pay for the vehicle and the petrol—that's every time a convoy goes over. It's extremely expensive. But to date, we've taken more than four million pounds worth of aid. And I know that's because of the Lord. He's opened so many doors.

I've learned a lot over the last four years. I've learned that as individuals, each of us can make a big difference, regardless of how small we are or how insignificant we think we are. I'm just an ordinary English housewife who got involved in this crazy adventure. I have put my hand out in times of real difficulty and I know that someone has physically taken it. And so I've learned to love my Savior very much. And it's been quite an incredible experience.

Interview by James Kimball and Kent Miles
March 7, 1997
Salt Lake City, Utah

Eleven Years Later

My last convoy to the Balkans was in 1999. In 2000, I was invited by LDS Humanitarian Services to visit Africa. We flew to Ghana to assess the situation and see if we could help in any way. I'll never forget that first trip.

I always had a dream to build an orphanage in Africa. It would be like a home with a momma and a family. There are so many children who grow up without their parents due to the AIDS epidemic, other diseases, and poverty. I wanted to give these children an environment that would be as close as possible to being raised in a family.

I returned in 2001 and bought thirty-six acres of land. This was in an area of great need. The first necessity was to sink a well so that there would be water for the village and for our site. We then began building houses that would each accommodate ten to twelve children, a momma and another caregiver.

We called the site Mmofra Trom, which means "Children's Garden." It was an apt name that captured what we wanted for these children. The homes were opened in 2004, and since then I have been privileged to see so many young children come to live in our homes. When they arrive, they are often sad, frightened and timid. Every time I visit Ghana, it has been amazing to see the transformation. When I see the children again, they are smiling, laughing and playing, as all young children should. Their personalities are flourishing. Confidence just gleams in their eyes.

We tried to make the site as self-sufficient as possible. There is a fish farm, poultry, and a plantation to provide food. Each child is trained in a trade that will help them provide for themselves when they are adults.

In 2006, we opened the school, and from its small beginnings it has grown and flourished. It now hosts four hundred students. The next plans are for a medical center that will reach out to forty villages in the surrounding area. All the volunteers at Hugs International feel that Mmofra Trom is an oasis in Ghana. We will always try to shelter and protect those in need. It has been a wonderful blessing to be part of this experience.

Email interview by Kent Miles
October 23, 2008

ANGELA CUMMINGS *is one of the world's most sought-after jewelry designers. A German native, she came to the United States right out of design school and quickly began her career at Tiffany & Co. in New York. She soon had her very own product line for Tiffany and an exclusive counter display in its Manhattan shop. After leaving Tiffany, she and her husband, Bruce, operated their own successful jewelry company.*

Angela Cummings

Jewelry Designer and Business Owner
Salt Lake City, Utah

My father was wonderful. He was an enlightened father, in that he didn't exert his dreams on me, and he didn't pressure me to do what he thought I would do well. He wanted me to be an interpreter for the United Nations. He thought I would be brilliant at that. But I never had the heart to tell him that language is really hard for me. Even if I was able to be bilingual, it was only because of circumstances, not because that's where I was talented.

I was always very artistic. I'm adopted, and he knew that my biological mother was an artist, but he never told me that. I guess he thought, *What's the point of holding her back if this is what she's going to do?* It seemed to be the one thing I excelled in, so he allowed me to pursue my studies.

In those days there were few formal jewelry designers. I was in Germany, and designing jewelry was not really a job. But in America it was different. Somehow, with a remarkable stroke of luck, I got a job at Tiffany & Co. Because I was so young, I didn't ask for anything. I was humble and enthusiastic. I had this German portfolio that was extremely meticulous—that's how they are there—so that's how I got the job.

I started as an assistant to the designers. There were two of them, and it was my job to help them with whatever they needed. That was my job for the first three years or so. Gradually, I started my own collection. In the meantime, I met Bruce, who had also moved to New York and worked at Tiffany. We were married about two years later. I don't know how romantic that is, but that's what happened.

I worked at Tiffany for eighteen years. Toward the end of my tenure, the company went through some major changes. It was sold to Avon, and with that sale the whole work environment changed. It became much more oriented toward mass production and classical design. When you're an artist or designer, you're not interested in classical design because that's all been done. Plus, there was a lot of office politics. It was messy.

So Bruce and I decided it was a good time to leave, and he left a year before I did. We mulled over what we were going to do, and I said, "Look, this is a good time to go into our own business." So that's what we did. I talked to our bishop for some business advice and he said this: "Don't try to build a house, have a baby, and start a business all at the same time." I had neglected to tell him that we were already in the process of building a house and having a baby, but it was still good advice.

In hindsight, I can see what he meant, but it was a special time. There was more to do than one ought to, but it was a great experience because you realize you can do anything, really, if you just gear up the energy to do it. If you can do that and have a positive mind, it will work. It was a year of very hard work.

~

What drives me to create? It's funny, but it's sort of like a little vacation from life. I'm up there in my studio and I can think of anything. It's like playing. I love the rest of my life, but I tune it all out. Then I come downstairs and I have to pick up my son, I have to think about dinner, I have to do this and that. When I hear women complain about how hard they work at home, I always tell them, "You know, when I go to the office it's like my vacation, and when I come home I have to work."

It's fun to be creative. It's a joy. But to be honest, as much as I love what I do, it has a place in my life. It isn't my all-consuming passion. I can put it away if I have to. There are other things to do that are more important in my life. So I'll drop it for a while because I know I can.

There are other things to think about. I'm struggling with my son's education right now. What to do that's best for him? That's more important to me. I'm in the lucky position where I don't have a boss who I need to explain this to. I know from other women that nobody really cares about your personal problems. They just don't. In my office, I do care when people have personal problems. Bruce and I pride ourselves on not running your typical office. We do get involved with peoples' personal lives, and we try to help them when they need it. Some people just need a little help and then everything's fine, so I do care when someone says they have a problem. But I know that in general nobody cares.

People work very hard in this country. But to learn, for instance, to make a piece of jewelry, you have to go to school for three-and-a-half years. Honestly, by the time you're a master jeweler, you could almost be a doctor. In our society, the perception is that doctors are more prestigious than jewelers. Few people are motivated to become master craftsmen because it's not socially rewarded in this country. If you're on Wall Street, even if you're dumb, you're in much higher esteem than if you're an absolutely brilliant goldsmith. The brilliant goldsmith is probably making more money than the dumb Wall Street exec, but few people know that because the good ones are very, very expensive.

The goldsmith is also giving a certain amount of beauty to the world. Our society just doesn't have a good way to measure that. It's hard to find kids who are willing to go through the learning process. It's even happening in New York. They're having staffing problems. In the meantime, computers are taking over our lives and it seems so old-fashioned to be a goldsmith. And yet, a computer cannot make a piece of jewelry.

A few years ago the big fashion of the moment was crosses. Everybody was wearing these big, jeweled crosses. It was immediately clear to me that this was *not* the direction to go. You don't go around with a sacred symbol and use it for fashion. Those two things are not compatible. That never used to be clear to me before I converted to Mormonism. It's hard to explain to people, such as department store heads, who say, "You know, the big thing is going to be crosses. You should do some."

I think copying someone else's designs is a real illness that is far too prevalent these days. Imitators don't realize how they're hurting the original artist. People lift from my designs, and it's a problem, but I've never pursued it legally because the laws aren't written to protect the artist. It's hard to get protection through the law. So rather than fight all the time and be negative, I don't worry about it.

I didn't know that I was adopted until I was in my early thirties. My father told me just before he died. Mom and Dad were always my parents, and they were such good parents. I feel strongly about this. Still, if my biological mother ever approached me, I wouldn't be upset by it.

I never questioned being adopted. In my parents' generation they never told their kids, so you never knew. I don't know if that's right or wrong, but I never felt adopted. When my father told my sister and me that we were both adopted, I wasn't upset. But my sister didn't respond to the news so well. I said to her, "Why are you so upset? We are lucky that these people adopted us. Who knows what our lives would have been like if they hadn't?"

Having a child—my son, Bruce—was an enormous change. But it only did me good. It put everything in perspective. Work is nice, but it has its place in your life. You see everything differently when you have the responsibility of parenthood.

When people in the Church are worried about women working and having children, I understand where they're coming from. I've had to make a lot of adjustments in my life in order to raise a child. I can't work nine to five; I wouldn't dream of doing that. You just can't do it. One parent has to be there whenever the child needs them. Not every minute, but certain times you have to be there, knowing that your children are more important than your job.

Having a child gave me a different perspective on design, too. It had to—all of my life experiences influence my work. Having to put myself at a child's level helps me to see things simplified. And that's a wonderful lesson —to appreciate seeing things the way a child sees them. I love to hear my son talk about what he observes. When adults look at things, we've often made up our minds how it looks before we even see it. But a child sees it for the first time.

We took him to the Caribbean once, and the first thing he said was, "That water's so blue!" And we know that water's blue, but we don't *see* it. It doesn't do to us the same thing it did to him. That color *is* incredible, come to think of it!

～

I often think of my life as *Before the Church* and *After the Church*. It's sort of like before and after you were married; it's that important, probably more so. Life in the Church has taught me to be fearless, to never be afraid of any change because it's not that important in the eternal perspective of things. Whatever happens in my business is not that big of a deal. And so I can be fearless. I don't mean reckless, because I worry about family. You don't want to pull the rug out from under your family on purpose, and it can happen even if it's not on purpose.

I have come to realize that when your life is perfect, you tend to get spiritually lazy. We don't have to fear the difficulties in life. It is during the hard times that God gives us more insight and more love.

I have a sense of being given a gift. I know a lot of designers around the world, and one of the biggest problems I see is ego. When you realize that you've been given a gift, it's only natural that you should use it in the best way you can. But you always have to remember it's a *gift*. There's no point in bragging about it because it was given to you; it's not like you earned it. I was born this way, and doing this is just one gift of many. I'm just lucky enough to recognize the things I do well. A lot of people have a gift and they don't ever discover it. They don't get a chance to realize it.

I often think, *Why am I doing this? There's enough jewelry in this world!* But if God wanted me to do something else he would have given me another gift. He wouldn't have given me this one. What can I do? I can't be an engineer because I just could never do it. I don't have the mind for it.

I know a lot of women in my age group who are divorced and who are leading meaningful lives. And alternately, there are divorced women who are bitter. I always think that I could have remained single, too. I just happened to meet Bruce. I don't know if I would have married if I hadn't met him. That's another gift—to be given a mate. Either you meet that person or you don't. How can anyone hold it against you if you don't? Maybe that's the challenge you're supposed to have in life? My father always said to me, "Whatever you do, don't just get married. I want you to have a career and be able to support yourself so that if anything ever happened in your marriage you'll be able to function." I think that's important.

Sometimes young women in the Church are groomed to become good wives. But you should be groomed to be a good human being. I don't think it matters what sex you are, you just have to be groomed to be good! If you have a relationship like marriage, you're forced to learn a lot of things you might not otherwise. You're forced to compromise and sacrifice, whether you like it or not. When you're single you have other challenges. You have to cope with being outgoing and making friends and having other kinds of relationships, which is also difficult. But I don't think your salvation depends on whether or not you're married. Who has control over that?

Bruce and I were just talking about the stereotype that Mormon men try to dominate their wives and daughters. I have never once felt that anyone in the Church was trying to limit my possibilities. Sure, there are some men who dominate their wives, but men do that in every culture. There are Catholic men, Protestant men, Muslim men who do that. Men have weaknesses and women have weaknesses. So it is not part of the Church. It is just part of the weaknesses of being men and women, and the Church gets the blame.

~

When I first met Bruce I didn't know anything at all about the Church. I was a Catholic who wasn't going to church and Bruce was a committed Mormon. But he was wonderful. He was never pushy about the Church, and I was convinced you could be of two different religions and live happily ever after. I suppose you can, but religion wasn't an issue between us.

By visiting Salt Lake often, I gradually learned about the Church. Bruce had daughters from a previous marriage, and since they were Mormon, I felt it was my duty to make sure they went to church. So I went to church with everybody, but I never committed to anything. Then one day our bishop asked me, sort of in a kidding way, "Why don't you just read the Book of

Mormon?" I think I had been complaining about the fact that we were always having these religious discussions, and I didn't always get it. That was frustrating. He said, "Just read it and you'll understand what everyone's talking about."

So I did. I read it, and I was very moved. Right away, I thought, *This is true. I can just tell it is true.* But it really worried me because I knew it was a big commitment. I don't think it's that difficult now, but in those days I was intimidated.

I hadn't wanted to know if it was true because once you *know* something you have to act on it. So I was straddling the fence. Then our son was born, and that was a big turning point. Now I had a son, and now I had to really think about the Chruch. I wanted him to have a rich spiritual life, and in order to nurture it in him I was going to have to be spiritual myself. Otherwise, I couldn't do it. I knew I had to be baptized and take the next step. In fact, I was already going to church and paying tithing, so everyone thought I was already a Mormon.

One day we were in our bishop's office, and he casually said, "It sure would be nice if you were baptized sometime." This was years after I read the Book of Mormon. We all laughed it off. But when we came home, I don't know what struck me, but all of a sudden I just got up and said to Bruce, "I know what it takes to get baptized. I don't want a big deal. I just want it done quickly and quietly." And so I did it. Then I knew I was committed and there was no going back. And I've never, ever regretted it.

Being Mormon has had a profound influence on how I approach my work. I don't fret about it any more. I used to worry if it was good enough or if I had spent enough time on it. Now I only go up to my studio when I have something specific to do. And I just go do it and finish it. I don't worry about it, and I don't really care if anyone likes it or not. We'll figure that out fast enough. If no one buys it, we won't make any more; that's all there is to it.

It's the same in life. When I dealt with people I always used to worry, *Oh, what are they going to think? I better word it this way.* I really don't fret about that any more. I just say it the way I see it. It works so much better. You don't waste time. And good people appreciate it.

～

When I was younger, I tried out for glee club. My sister, who is a pretty good singer, looked at me and said, "Don't ever sing. You're off-key." I was at a delicate age, and I never opened my mouth to sing again. But as soon as I was baptized, I don't know what happened, but I was able to sing. It's the strangest thing, I was no longer afraid of being off-key. It's not that I have a great voice, but singing suddenly became a pleasure in my life again.

Interview by James Kimball and Kent Miles
February 1, 1997
Greenwich, Connecticut

Eleven Years Later

You can never really see the end from the beginning. I never imagined I'd achieve the things I did in the jewelry business. I never imagined I'd marry a Mormon and become one myself. I never imagined New York would experience the devastation of 9/11, or the tragic effects of the economic collapse. I never imagined that my husband, Bruce, would develop lymphoma or that we'd be living in Utah. But you deal with the changes and work to solve each day's problems. The problems we face continually change, and that is the essence of creativity. Creativity is problem solving.

After 9/11, we decided to close our business. Everyone in Manhattan had a couple of terrible business years and it seemed like a good time to close up shop. Bruce had always wanted to return to live in Utah. He would not have imposed that on us, but I knew it was something he wanted. He was diagnosed with lymphoma, and I wanted to make what remaining time we had together pleasant. Our son loves Utah and was delighted at the idea of living here.

It turned out to be a good thing to move here. I'm still working, but not at the level I was before. That has been a challenge: how to be creative without the framework of business and the art of designing jewelry. You know, artists tend to look at their art as a wonderful thing, but it is not everything. As good as we might be at creating beautiful things, the world isn't usually moved by it that much—not as much as we would like to think.

~

My birth mother had been trying to find me for many years. Finally, after a rather tortuous journey, she made contact. She wrote me a letter through an attorney who was a friend of the family. He contacted me and said, "There's an elderly lady who'd like to contact you." I thought it was probably someone who wanted to return a piece of jewelry! So I wrote her a nice letter, and she replied, telling me she was my birth mother. Absolutely out of the blue!

She asked if we could meet. When I was finally able to respond, I arranged to meet her during a trip to Europe. I didn't want to involve my family until I knew more about her. We were to meet at the Frankfurt airport. My husband said, "How are you ever going to find her there? That airport is huge!" I said, "Don't worry. We'll find each other." When I got off the plane, I saw her immediately. She looked just like me, only older.

It turned out she was a designer, had been all her life. She gave me my genealogy all the way back to the sixteenth century. She also gave me a picture of one of my great-great-grandfathers. He actually was a jewelry designer. Believe it or not, he went to the same design school in Germany that I attended. And there were artists and sculptors among my ancestors. It explained why I was always drawn to art and design. I was very close to my parents, but they were professional people. As a child, I was drawing all the time, something they never did. Once I met my birth mother, I could tell this was the family from which my artistic nature came. She was so much like me in every way. Her house looked like a smaller version of my house. We had the same tastes and wore the same kinds of clothes. We even had the same hair cut!

So when I met her it changed me. It had a big impact on my interest in genealogy—in my ancestors and those who came before us. I had never cared much about ancestry before. But since learning more about my genealogy, I have tried to pass that along to my son. It's a way to balance out the powerful ancestors he has on his father's side. They came across the plains with the Mormon pioneers.

Learning about family makes you start to think outside of yourself more. You see yourself as more connected. Before that, I was more involved in myself. This reconnection with my family made me feel part of something bigger. And in a way, it makes you smarter. It makes you open to hearing things and keeps you from becoming too wrapped up in yourself.

I knew that I had been adopted. I just didn't know about my birth family heritage. But all of the good things that happened in my life came because I was adopted. If I hadn't been adopted I might never have come to the States. I might still be in Germany, or in South Africa, where many of my birth family ended up. I would never have met Bruce and perhaps never joined the Church.

I can't imagine what my life would have been like had I not been adopted. My father was worried that when I learned the truth it would change my feelings for him. I told him, "Daddy, it makes me love you even more, especially when I think that in those terrible days in Germany at the end of World War II, you were willing to take on the responsibility of raising a baby!" That was a real big leap of love. He did so much for me. He was responsible for all the opportunities that came to me. So meeting my birth mother did not cause me to feel I had lost anything. Meeting her was a gift that added to my life.

Interview by Kent Miles
August 13, 2008
Salt Lake City, Utah

MARIA CONSUELO DIMAYA *was a member of a guerilla group in the Philippines during the 1970s, fighting against the authoritarian Marcos regime. She worked as a medic and met her husband shortly before leaving the opposition. Today, she is an active member of the LDS Church who has held almost every position open to women in her ward. She currently teaches geriatric/pediatric caregiving and is earning a post-graduate degree in order to teach English as a second language in the Philippines. She goes by the nickname Chelito, which means "Little Heaven."*

Maria Consuelo Dimaya

Former Guerilla Medic, Teacher
Santa Rosa, Laguna, Philippines

I was born on September 12, 1951, in Nasipit Agusan del Norte. It is a small town on Mindanao.[1] I've been a member of the LDS Church for almost twenty-seven years and I have a sister who was baptized this year. I have nine children—seven are living, I lost two in infancy—and one granddaughter. I have one son who's on a mission in California right now, and two children studying at BYU-Hawaii. My oldest son went to BYU and met his wife there. They're now living in Midvale, Utah. The rest of my children are still living at home.

Although I was born on Mindanao, I was raised in Manila, the capital of the Philippines.

---

1. Mindanao is one of the three main islands of the Philippines.

After I was born my father went to work for the U.S. naval base at Subic Bay, and from there he went to Pakistan and Vietnam as a civilian employee.

I grew up Catholic. I studied in an exclusive girls' school and later transferred to a private high school. Afterward, I went to the University of Santo Tomas and studied nursing for three years. I never took it up as a profession, because in 1972 I got involved with a movement that was fighting against the Marcos[2] dictatorship. I became involved because my cousin, whom I was rooming with, was a leader of the MAKIBAKA. This was a woman's organization that was the counterpart to the men's organization opposing Marcos.

There were lots of anti-Marcos discussion groups meeting in the schools, and they were particularly interested in recruiting from the college of nursing so they could staff the movement's medical units. My cousin asked me to help her with a few minor tasks—typing her speeches and proofreading some of their literature. Of course, when you're proofreading you're also reading. I started thinking, *This is really something important*, and I started going to meetings with her.

I recognized that there were social problems in my country. I saw poverty all around me every day. But I thought, *Well, that's life. There's nothing you can do about it.* As I grew up and went to college and read my cousin's

2. Ferdinand Emmanuel Edralín Marcos (1917–1989), president of the Philippines from 1965 to 1986. His authoritarian rule was characterized by human rights abuses and corruption.

literature, I realized that you *can* do something about it. I decided that it wouldn't be enough to finish college and go to work, helping my family and myself. You have to help others as well. So I decided to join my cousin in the movement and I participated in rallies and demonstrations against Marcos.

My cousin was blacklisted by the government and had to leave school. She told me, "If anything happens, don't worry, we'll get you out of here." Not long afterwards, following a major demonstration, I was blacklisted and jailed, too.

My father did not visit me in jail, nor did he bail me out for fear of associating with me. He was worried about traveling abroad for his job. The school expelled me, saying it couldn't be responsible for my actions. When I was released, the police followed me everywhere. My cousin contacted me and said the movement would pick me up and take me into the underground. I wound up in a safe house in Manila, and that's where I met my husband.

We learned that we would both be sent to Angeles City, Pampanga, to staff a hospital that was being built by the Communist Party of the Philippines (CPP). When we reached Angeles, we started buying medicines and supplies for the hospital. We worked with the doctors in the operating room, learning first aid procedures, but at the same time we were providing support for the CPP and its military wing, the New People's Army (NPA). Any of their people who were wounded in encounters with the military were sent to us. We treated them for gunshot wounds, many of them serious, because the government troops used soft-nosed bullets that make a small entry wound but leave a large, nasty exit wound.

After a while, my husband was sent to the mountains, where more people were being shot. There were also many cases of tuberculosis and other diseases. I was already pregnant with our first child and I stayed behind in the city, running the hospital. What I didn't know was that one of our patients had been caught by the government and tortured. He told me later that the soldiers broke one of his legs. He finally gave in to the pain and told them where the hospital was located.

One afternoon I was alone at the hospital and I locked it up to take a nap. Somehow the troops broke in and I was awakened by a gun barrel poking me in the face. A man's voice behind the gun shouted, "Wake up!" Ten men in army uniforms surrounded me and I panicked.

"No sudden movements," they told me. "Just stand up and turn around." They were looking for one of our commanders and I told them, "He's not here. Go ahead and look around, but there's no one here but me." When they searched the attic they found the guns we were hiding for protection.

"What's this?" they asked me.

"Well, we have them for protection," I said. "Come on, I can't even reach the attic."

Often female prisoners were raped or even killed, but for some reason they didn't touch me. I was using the *nom de guerre* of a prominent and wealthy person and they might have thought they would be in trouble if anything happened to me. But I still didn't escape torture. I think everyone had to undergo that. I was beaten with the stock of an M16 rifle. They wanted me to tell them where my husband was.

While they decided what to do with me, my commander came back to the hospital. He came back because he heard that our former patient had been captured. He wanted to get me out of the hospital before the troops got there. When he came in, they grabbed him and started beating both of us. The commander kept shouting, "Don't touch her!" But the more he shouted, the more they beat him. They wanted him to give evidence against me, but he refused.

After we were beaten they took us to the military camp in Angeles, Camp Olivas, for tactical interrogation. They asked me questions, and if I didn't give the answer they wanted to hear, they slapped me. I still withheld my real name, so my parents never learned that I had been taken.

I finally had to tell the military that I was pregnant with my first baby. They sent me to a hospital to make sure that the beatings hadn't damaged my baby. Luckily, everything was fine.

When I got back from the hospital, they kept me in a military barracks with the other female prisoners. We were fed dried fish and rice, which wasn't enough nourishment for a healthy baby. But the people outside brought fresh fruits and vegetables to the prisoners, and thanks to them my first son was born perfectly healthy.

After the birth of my first child, we lived in the prison for another year. I applied for amnesty on the grounds that prison wasn't a healthy place to raise an infant. After a series of conferences, the military agreed to grant me amnesty on the condition that I report in weekly. They wanted to make sure the child was well and I was no longer with the opposition. My husband heard through sources in the underground that I had been released and sent me a note saying he wanted to see our son for the first time. He knew the risks, but he was just too excited about being a father to stay away.

Eventually we managed to set up a meeting. The baby cried the entire time, but my husband was thrilled. He promised to find a way we could all be together again in the underground. One day he sent word that I should pack my belongings and meet him at a certain time and place. I went there and waited, but he never came. I learned through friends that he had been taken prisoner and was being tortured. Even today, he still feels some pain as a result of his beatings in prison.

～

My husband was held prisoner for eight months. After he was freed we went to Cebu City, where his family lived. We tried to find work, but no one would hire him because he was a known opponent of the Marcos regime. My husband is quite an artist, and he started giving art lessons and selling his own paintings. Eventually he had several students and that's how we got by.

It was about this time that we first became acquainted with the LDS Church. My husband's cousin was working for the LDS Church Educational System, and he was transferred to Cebu to help establish the Seminary program there. He and his wife told us a little about the Church. Later, we met the missionaries when they began coming by to meet with my father-in-law.

Eventually my father-in-law lost interest, but the missionaries still came by. They would play with my baby and I would sit and chat with them. Soon my husband joined us, and before long we were listening to the discussions. About a year-and-a-half later, in 1975, we were both baptized.

After we were baptized, some people from the guerilla movement contacted us to see how we felt about becoming involved with the opposition again. We told them, "We have two kids now. We still support the goals of the movement, but we'll support them in a way that seems best for us and our children." We found that the Church gave us opportunities to work to improve the social conditions in our country. One of the most important factors in changing the culture of poverty is the change that is made inside a person, and the Church showed us that if you have the desire to make that change, everything outside will change too.

My husband and I served a mission in Tacloban City, in the Visayan Islands. It's a beautiful part of the Philippines and it made me proud to be a citizen of such a lovely country. The Philippines is a great place to live, if you know how to live properly. So many of the people are poor and illiterate, and the help they receive from the government and other sources doesn't really show them how they can make things better for themselves. Being an active Church member helps you see a better way.

The Church makes a big difference in people's lives here. I think the

Church welfare program is the best in the Philippines. I see this in my ward, where we have many indigent members. Our bishop is a good man and he finds a way to help everybody. During the recent flooding here, it took the government some time to respond, but the Church was there right away. Even non-members got assistance from the Church.

Back in 1979, our house burned down. After that and the floods, my husband says, "Well, now we can sing, 'I've seen fire, and I've seen rain.'" That fire was the first big trial we went through after joining the Church, but it was much harder to deal with the loss of our two children who died in infancy. My visiting teachers were a source of support during those times, and I continued to read the scriptures. Ultimately, I relied on my faith in God and the knowledge that I would see my children again if I remained faithful and true.

I'd like to see young women working to change the world, but I'd like to see them use a different approach than the one I used in my twenties. Back then, I saw the opposition making a difference in people's lives, but when the government captured us, the local people went back to the lives they led before. They hadn't changed inside. If more young people would share their testimonies with others, help them see how they can change the way they look at themselves and others, that would make a real difference.

I'm not sure how well young people here are receiving the gospel message. I've been to Church dances where I saw young people dancing to music with objectionable lyrics—lyrics that would drag them down instead of edifying them. And I see young people dressing in ways that reflect fashion more than the attitudes of a gospel lifestyle. Part of that, I'm sure, is just normal peer pressure and adolescent rebellion, but another part of the problem is that practically all of the Church materials we receive are in English. If you don't speak English well, then it's difficult to get the full gospel message here. I'm concerned that we're losing a lot of young people because of this problem.

Parents bear the biggest responsibility for keeping their children on the gospel path. They can express the gospel in their family life—through family prayers, family home evening, and their own conduct. Always watch for those "teaching moments." They don't always occur in the chapel.

I taught Seminary for eighteen years and LDS Institute[3] for two years. That experience taught me so much. In fact, I've learned more through my experiences in the Church than I ever did from my experiences in the hills. In the hills, you woke up every day, thinking, *Today I might die.* My cousin, who got me involved with the opposition, did die. It was even more terrifying to think that someday I might have to kill someone so that I could survive. None of that applies in the Church. Instead, you always find new opportunities to express your love for others and to bask in God's love.

If I could give young women in the Philippines one piece of advice, it would be to stay close to the Church. It may not be able to solve all of your

---

3. Religious educational classes for young members of the LDS Church; usually located near high schools and universities, respectively.

problems, but it can keep you on the right path. Adhering to the principles of the gospel is the one sure way to happiness, and it will never lead you astray.

Interview by Kent Miles
November 6, 2000
Manila, Philippines

Eight Years Later

I still have three children at home. Another two are in college and one just left for his mission. I have married children. I'm happy they married in the temple and remained strong in the Church. Our children like the stories we tell from the revolution, but their experiences have been those of growing up in the Church. They have learned to be independent, and I have seen them make their own difficult decisions based upon the values they have received from the Church. When I think of independence in terms of our experience in the revolution, it is very, very different from the kind of independence my children have grown up with.

As my kids grew older I was able to do my housework much more quickly. I found I had more time on my hands. So I decided to go back to college and get additional training in the care of geriatric/pediatric patients. I completed that study and after six months my school hired me to teach caregiving.

I started teaching, and soon I decided I should improve myself some more. I enrolled in college to get a bachelor of arts in communication with a major in English. I decided on English because eventually I'd like to teach it as a second language to non-English speakers—like Chinese, Koreans, Japanese, and of course, Filipinos.

This has a connection with my other work. Many students in my care-giving classes cannot speak English well, which makes it much more difficult to find employment. I just graduated with my bachelor's degree, and in order to teach English as a second language I will need to take additional courses that will be equivalent to getting a master's degree. So that is what I start on next. Life is never dull.

The biggest surprise I have had in life, since the time I had children, was the way they suddenly grew up, got married, and left home. It was as though I woke up one day and my children suddenly had their own families. I have come to realize that life is short and our experiences here on earth teach us what God wants us to learn. Nothing is permanent in this world. The only permanency is change.

Telephone interview by Kent Miles
October 5, 2008

LEA ROSSER *is currently a senior executive in the government of New South Wales, Australia. After struggling in grade school, she excelled in higher education, earning four degrees, including a master of business and a master of arts. She became a librarian, an amateur genealogist, and eventually the city manager of Auburn, Australia, an area of Sydney where many of the Olympic events were held in 2000.*

Lea Rosser

City Manager, Auburn, Australia
Auburn, Australia

There is a book called *Spiritual Serendipity*, by Richard Eyre.[1] He talks about this fable by Horace Walpole called "The Three Princes of Serendip." Serendip is the Persian name for Sri Lanka. The fable is about this old king with three sons, all of whom were vying to wear the crown after their father died. The king sent them out on a quest, each with a specific target to reach, and whoever succeeded would be worthy to become king.

---

1. *Spiritual Serendipity: Cultivating and Celebrating the Art of the Unexpected* (Simon and Schuster, 1997)

As they travelled, each prince stopped along the way to help people. When their time was up, they each realized that they hadn't achieved what their father had sent them out to do. They returned home and said to their dad, "We failed you, we haven't done what you wanted us to do." And he said, "No, you haven't failed. By doing those other things, you fulfilled the goal I sent you out to achieve." And that's where the word serendipity comes from, where you adapt and take advantage of the unplanned circumstances that come your way.

The position I'm in now is because unplanned circumstances arose, and I've been fortunate enough to recognize them as opportunities. It's just unfolded as it has. By doing that, I've also allowed the things necessary for me to get here to have occurred, so I can do what's required of me.

I like that word, "serendipity," it's a nice-sounding word. It pretty well sums up what's happened in my life. I grew up in a country town. We moved there when I was three. We were the only members of the LDS Church in our town, and we traveled to Canberra to go to church—a forty-mile drive. When we arrived, it was a tiny branch with three other families. We were the fourth.

Living in that town, you really had to know that the Church was true. It was a traditional country town. You were either Catholic, Methodist, or Church of England, and if you weren't one of those then there was something peculiar about you. I got a lot of bad treatment. I have a brother four years older than me, and at school we were treated differently. We were often bashed up, and our friends would join the other kids when we walked home. Even though I was very young, it really made me stop and wonder what it was all about and whether it was worth it. In those early days, there had to be something about the Church that held me to the standards, even under those adverse circumstances. It must have been a testimony of the gospel. I knew it was true. I always felt very comfortable with the Church.

We couldn't always get to church because our car wouldn't work or we wouldn't have enough money for petrol. When that happened, Mum would always read us stories out of the scriptures or tell us about the Mormon pioneers. She had old Primary[2] and Sunday School lesson manuals, and she would read us stories out of those, and I would think, *Well, if the pioneers can do it . . .*

At school, I studied French because I thought it would be nice to speak a language. I was only there for about six weeks when they pulled me out of class and said, "You can't do French any more. We've put you into woodwork." Well, the impression everyone had of woodwork was that it was for people who couldn't do anything. I asked why, and they said, "Because your Australian accent is so strong you will never speak French." So I was put into woodwork. But I recognized it as an opportunity and I had a wonderful time.

In Australia, if you want to go to university you have to do six years of high school. If you don't do university, then you leave school after your fourth year, around age sixteen. I wasn't very good at school. I got to the end

---

2. A religious education program for LDS children ages three through twelve.

of my fourth year and my dad said he would take me to go and study to be a secretary. My mum said to me, "No, if you want to go and do a fifth and sixth year, you go ahead. You can do it if you really want."

Instead, I went off to business college on Saturdays to learn how to type, but I didn't last very long. I had played the piano and I couldn't quite understand why you can't use different fingers on the different keys of the typewriter, like you can on the piano. I was a bit of a dropout after a few weeks. They said to me, "You just can't play tunes on those keys."

So I took Mum's advice and encouragement and stayed on for fifth and sixth levels. I passed and got admission to three universities. My brother was already at university and was preparing to go on his mission. My parents couldn't afford to have me at university and him on a mission at the same time. So he went to Tahiti and I went to work.

Australia had open exams for employment with the Commonwealth Public Service. You'd get work for four months, and at the end of that time they would usually offer you a permanent job. I passed the exam and got a job with the Department of Defense in Canberra. I stayed with it for a couple of months, but it was just terrible. You'd get your week's work issued on Monday and it was supposed to last you the whole week. We'd have it finished by 10:00 or 11:00 that same day. You'd go and ask for more work and there wasn't any. I wasn't going to stick around *this* for the rest of my life.

I applied for three jobs listed in the paper and decided that I would take the first one that opened up. Then I got a letter offering me a job in a library I had applied to earlier. So I only had about a week to pack up and come up to Sydney to start working. That was my first real job.

There is no doubt that the Lord led me on the course he wanted me to go. I wasn't very good in school, and it wasn't because I was dumb. It was just that my brother was very good—he always came in first in everything. He's quite different from me and he learns differently than I do. Being in a small town, the teachers assumed that I was the same as him, that I would learn the same and be as good at the same subjects. Being different from him, I guess I got a bit shortchanged on my education.

When I left school there were two or three things I wanted to be. I wanted to be an art teacher. I wanted to be a back-up singer in a band, singing for somebody like Linda Ronstadt. I thought I'd like to be a chemist (called a pharmacist in America). You see, I'm quite tall and I used to fall over a lot. I ended up spending a lot of my time at the chemist's buying bandages, so I had this affinity for the chemist's shop.

When I started working at the library, there were some new librarians fresh from university. I used to listen to them talk about what they had learned, and I realized that although they had been to university, they didn't have as much knowledge as I had. I thought, *Boy, if they can go to university and pass and come out and be librarians, goodness me, so can I!*

So I went off and enrolled in an extended study for a library degree.

Once I started I thought I'd better get this done as quickly as possible. So I took some business subjects because they were worth more units than any of the others. If I took enough of those, I could finish in four years instead of six. Once I started doing these business subjects I realized that there were some particular areas that I did very well in. So when I finished my library degree I decided to go right back and get my business degree. That caused me to start looking outside the library for other opportunities and challenges. It really has just been serendipity—taking advantage of circumstances as they've come along.

As I've gone from one job to another, I've learned something at each stage that has been key in the next. I've picked up a new skill or talent in one job, and that's the skill or talent they need in the next job. But my progress has been at some cost. I just completed my third degree, and all three have been done while working full-time, so it's been at a considerable cost of personal time. I've had to study a lot harder than some others. It's only as I've done my last degree that I've really understood how to study and how to think differently.

I've also tried to make sure that my studying hasn't detracted from church. I think it would be easy to find an excuse, to say, *Well, I've only got X number of hours in the day and this is more important than that.* For some people, church always seems to be the first thing to go. So I've always tried to make it the first priority. In doing that, there's always been time to do everything else that I've needed to do.

It's been a sacrifice for my parents because they have had to put up with me, sitting up all night finishing assignments. I remember when I was doing my business degree at a university about six hundred miles south of Sydney. I had a major assignment that had to be in on Tuesday or else I'd fail my whole degree. It *had* to be in. I had it all written out by hand, but I hadn't typed it. So my Dad sat up all night on the word processor, and as I finished writing, he typed it up. He's the one that should have gone and been a secretary!

We finished it at six o'clock in the morning, and then he jumped on the bus, pushed himself into the central railway station and caught the seven o'clock train. It was an all-day trip and he got there at a quarter past four that afternoon. The office had closed at four, so he went around the campus and found somebody to open up the office so he could hand in this last assignment for me.

I've been very blessed with wonderful parents who have made great sacrifices. They've assisted financially, buying textbooks and things, because librarians aren't paid good money. They've always taken the approach that if somebody was doing something in the family, then we all helped. That's become our philosophy: if somebody's working on something and they need to get it done and they need help, then we all pitch in and we all work together so it can be done. Whatever it takes, we do it.

⌒

Some may feel I have had a career at the expense of being married. I see it in another light. The circumstances in my life have been such that I haven't had the opportunity to be married. But that is not to say that I have not been dealt many other blessings. I have been blessed to teach young women in Primary and become Primary president. Then I advised some of the same girls in Young Women.[3] I was blessed to serve as their stake Young Women president and then as their stake Relief Society president. And now I am blessed to see them serve in their church callings.

I would rather have had children of my own, but as I've watched these women and seen their lives unfold, nothing has given me greater satisfaction. I know that I've had a small part in helping them become who they are.

It is sad that some people feel that your time on earth isn't fulfilled if you aren't married. Some feel there isn't a role, or a place in the Church, for single sisters. Our opportunities are without end and our spheres of influence are unencumbered. There are so many opportunities and so many things than can be accomplished with our lives.

I have no doubt that the Lord led me on the course he wanted, both in the best of times and the worst of times. We all need to remember that we came to earth knowing what our lives would be like. We came here willingly and with great joy, knowing that we would have the opportunity to experience life. If we can remember that, it helps to put life's circumstances into perspective. We all have different talents; we need to make the most of the life God has given us. We need to take advantage of the moments the Lord hands us.

---

3. A youth organization for LDS girls ages twelve through eighteen.

About ten years ago, I became very ill. There was a terrible virus running around Sydney. People were dying because it would give them heart attacks . . . they'd just die. Because I get bad cases of asthma, the virus gave me a massive asthma attack instead of a heart attack. That was a blessing. A heart attack might have killed me. I was rushed to hospital and they pumped me full of cortisone to stop the attack. Now, unbeknownst to me, I'm allergic to cortisone. So while it fixed my asthma, it totally shut down my adrenal system. I wasn't able to work for about seven months afterward.

They said, "Oh, you just need a holiday."

I'm an avid reader, but after a month of reading, it was just too much sitting around all the time. I thought, *What can I do?* One day, Mum pulled out this huge case of letters from my great-grandmother. It's just this enormous suitcase with so much family history inside. I said to her, "While I'm in this state and not able to do anything, why don't I start sorting through the genealogy?"

So that's what we did for six months. We researched all the branches of our family tree back to the late 1600s. We've found more than fifteen hundred direct ancestors of the Rossers and their offshoots. They seem to fall out of the sky. We don't just get one name, they come in batches of a hundred or more. You can tell they're waiting for us. And even though I stayed horribly ill, we got it done.

It wasn't until Mum and I finished gathering the genealogy that the doctors figured out what was wrong with me. I went back to my doctor, got a little tablet that I had to take for two weeks, and I was back at work again. So I had enough time to gather these names, get them ready to be submitted to the temple, and then I was back at work. That's just how things happened.

It goes back to that fable about serendipity. I could have sat there for seven months thinking, *Woe is me! I think I'm going to die*, but I just didn't want to waste time. I've always had this kind of energy all my life, but as I got a little bit older I understood that I could use that energy to do things. When I was young I used to read a lot and I used to daydream. But as I got older—probably when I was about fourteen or fifteen—I started to understand things a little bit better. I realized that rather than just imagining and reading and dreaming, I could actually use that energy to make things happen.

Interview by James Kimball
February 23, 1997
Sydney, Australia

Photos by James Kimball

Eleven Years Later

I was with the Auburn City Council for the 2000 Olympic Games. The state was really the entity involved in organizing the Games. My job was not nearly so flashy, but it had a down-to-earth, long-term reality. It was to prepare for the strategic impact of the Games upon the growth of the community. There would be thousands of new residents moving here after the Olympics and we needed to make sure city services were prepared to accommodate them.

A year after the Olympics, I became the general manager of two city councils that merged into one. I had to plan for what would happen when those two organizations were brought together and administer the services that would be provided for the large population living in this new city of Canada Bay. There were about sixty thousand residents, with another twenty-five thousand expected to move in within a short time. It has been an adventure managing the expectations of the community and making sure they were not disadvantaged by the transition. And it's been challenging to bring two councils together and build a new civic culture. We created something new out of two existing organizations, and believe me, there was never a dull moment.

One of the interesting things about this job was working with the diversity of people moving into the community. It takes a lot for the long-time residents to understand and welcome the cultural change that newcomers bring. It's a lot like what we are seeing in the Church, with long-time members learning to embrace and understand new members who come from different backgrounds with different languages and traditions. The gospel provides a perspective that helps us see that what we have in common is greater than the differences that separate us.

Every day has its challenges. It's like in the Bible. Everyone has their seven years of plenty, followed by seven lean years. That's when the real test comes. There will be pain and sorrow. There will be highs and lows. There are times when we're working and our talents are being fully utilized, and there are times when we feel our experience is not being used. That's the time to make sure you're properly engaged during the interim and prepare for the time when things take off again.

When I was in school I never thought I'd be a career woman or that I'd be a government official. It has been very satisfying. But nothing has been gratifying in quite the same way as my church service. Years ago I was called to be our ward Primary president, and it was a shock to the other members to have a young, single woman called to that position. When my name was announced for a sustaining vote, you could hear the collective intake of breath from the congregation, they were so surprised.

My life's really an adventure. It is a serendipitous exercise. Whatever comes, I just think, *Okay, we're off! Let's see what the outcome will be.* I've had sad times and hard times and some really great times. It is really about the joy of the journey, and understanding that if we hang in there we will be right where we need to be at the end.

So for a girl who got thrown out of French and put into woodwork, who couldn't type because it wasn't like piano, who wasn't expected and couldn't afford to go to university, that knowledge has come in pretty handy. I've been able to get a master of business degree in addition to a bachelor of business and a bachelor of arts. I've been able to work in the administration of city governments. I was the executive manager of the Auburn Council, which hosted the Olympic Games.

Not bad for a country girl who was expelled from secretarial school.

Telephone interview by Kent Miles
October 3, 2008

VICTORIA FONG KESLER *is a homemaker and mother of twelve. The daughter of Chinese immigrants, she was given up for adoption at an early age. Throughout her life, she has overcome adversity through her strong personal faith and the support of her family. She is active in her ward, where she teaches, conducts music, works with Public Affairs, and was recently released as Relief Society president.*

Victoria Fong Kesler

Homemaker, Mother of Twelve
Rifle, Colorado

I was born December 14, 1952, in San Francisco, California. I don't know much about my background. As I have met with my natural family over the last fifteen years, I've gathered that my father's uncle was here in America, and he brought my father over from China. According to Chinese custom, he adopted my father into his family. So my father became that uncle's son. I have a second cousin who considers my father to be his brother and calls himself my uncle. How utterly confusing to me!

My father left his first family in China—a wife, a daughter and a son—and came over to the States to try to make a better life. Somewhere along the way, he met my mother, they became involved, and I was born. I remember little; of course, I was very young. My memories start when we moved to Provo, Utah.

My father wanted to get out of California, get away from the fast life. I don't know what made him choose Provo. My mother was a hostess and he was a cook, and they worked at a restaurant in Provo called the China City Cafe, on University Avenue. I was born in 1952, so they must have come between '54 and '56.

My mother didn't like Provo, it wasn't the lifestyle she was used to in San Francisco. I remember she was very, very stern. She loved babies, but as her children got older she grew intolerant. I know there was probably physical abuse—I found out later from half-brothers and -sisters that there had been. I remember her getting angry and pinching my arm severely if I said or did something that didn't please her.

Our apartment in Provo is still there. It had a window seat, and that's where I slept. I remember watching a neon light across the street. It was for a tire store, and I always watched as it flashed off and on at night. I remember little of my father. He seemed kind and gentle. When my mother wanted me to eat with chopsticks, he got me a spoon. That's about all I remember of my father from that time.

⁓

My mother met Donna at the China City Cafe—Donna was a waitress. My natural mother would bring me to the café, and Donna just fell in love with me. She thought I was the cutest thing she had ever seen. She already had four children of her own and was raising her niece. She often commented that if my mother ever wanted to give me away, they'd sure take me. Mother allowed Donna to bring me home to visit. I remember her blue overcoat and the purple dresses her daughters wore. I was perhaps three-and-a-half.

When I first went to live with Donna's family, I remember that they kept me kind of hidden. Once they got me, it was like they didn't want anybody to see me. When my big brother *would* take me places, we would go for car rides and he would keep me hidden down in the seat. But I remember how fun-loving he was. He was always kind and joked around with me.

For some reason, I was told there was another Chinese family that really wanted me, and my foster mom always said, "It's a good thing you didn't go with that family because they would have worked you to death." Those little comments I can vaguely remember.

We moved down to Beaver, Utah, and that's where I started going to kindergarten. Beaver was a small town, maybe two thousand people. I don't remember having any problems the first time we lived there, which was through the second grade. I got along well with the other kids. They thought it was really neat to have a Chinese girl living in the area—there were no other ethnic groups there, only myself. They would bring the Navajo children in as part of the Indian Placement Program,[1] but that wasn't the same.

---

1. An LDS program (1947–1996) through which Native Americans were encouraged to voluntarily place their children in Caucasian homes and schools.

Then we moved back to Provo, where I attended third, fourth and fifth grades. That's when I began to realize I was different. I was always with Caucasian children. There were no other Oriental people around me, other than those who rented apartments from my foster mother. It was funny when Chinese people would come to look at the apartments. When I'd answer the door they'd start speaking Chinese to me. I didn't have a clue how to speak Chinese. I probably understood it when I first came to my new family, but I speak none now, though I wish I did.

I had a few friends in Provo, but they always seemed to be the under-dogs, the kids who were frequently teased. I never got into the popular cliques. Then my foster mother moved us back to southern Utah—back to Beaver.

My foster mother's husband was in the picture, but I don't talk about him much. He was abusive. She divorced him when I was in the sixth grade. I hope I've forgiven him, but it's still a touchy subject. There was sexual abuse. My mother finally came to realize that something was going on, so she got rid of him. But nothing legally was ever done about the abuse. They took me to see some doctors, but that was about it.

So I felt different, and perhaps that's why I did some of the things I did. When I went back to Beaver in the sixth grade, I wasn't popular any more. Being Oriental was not a plus, as it turns out. I still remembered all the kids, and they remembered me, but they had their social cliques. It was just never the same. I never felt I had any good friends.

My family was not active in the LDS Church, but my foster sister encouraged my mother to let me go to Primary. She was married by then and had a baby and was trying to get to church herself. We only lived two blocks away from the chapel, so I'd walk to church and go to sacrament meeting[2] on Sunday and Primary after school.

As I grew older I became more active in the Church and I really enjoyed it. I remember going to the St. George Temple to do baptisms for the dead.[3] That was really great. I started feeling that's where I needed to be and that's what I needed to be doing. I always felt a presence, something beyond what I could see with my eyes. And I always felt that the Church was true, even though I wasn't baptized until I was twelve. I wasn't legally adopted, so it was kind of hard to know what to do. I went by my foster family's last name, but there were a few legal questions, so for Church records they ended up using my natural parents' name—Fong—as my middle name, followed by the foster name.

I rolled along through school and started to get a lot of teasing. I'd be called different names that were *not* complimentary. There were a lot of ethnic slurs, mostly by the boys. And the popular girls, the ones I had grown up with, they were cheerleaders, members of the pep club—I was never included.

My early teenage years were really hard. I was the last one at home.

2. The principal LDS Sunday service.
3. The practice of baptizing a living proxy who is standing in for a deceased person.

All my foster brothers and sisters are much older than I am; the closest is six years older. They were all married when I was going through my teens, and none of them ever knew about the ethnic problems I was having. I never came home and complained, "I'm being called this or that." My foster mother was busy just trying to keep us surviving. She had a big home that she could never give up. It took a lot to maintain it, so she was never around when I came home from school.

As I grew older I realized that you have two sides. One side says, *I'm never having children!* And the other says, *If I ever have children . . .* That's where I was: *Okay, whenever I have children, I'm not going to work so they don't have to come home and be alone.* That became one of my goals. Another was that I'd never divorce.

I met my husband in my junior year of high school. He had just come back from Vietnam. He was tough acting and good looking. As we started dating, the ethnic slurs and teasing quit. I distinctly remember walking into the school library and some boys started to bug me. One of them said clearly, so everyone could hear, "You better leave her alone. She goes with Stephen." You could have heard a pin drop. I have to admit, it was the greatest day ever because it was the end of the taunting and the mean things that were said.

It's strange. These kids who were teasing me were from good, active LDS families, but I'm not sure if the parents ever knew what their sons were saying. But Stephen did, and I didn't have any problems for the rest of high school, which was wonderful. I felt like he was my hero—he was the guy who took care of me, and has done so ever since.

We were married in December 1970, and moved to Milford, Utah (about thirty miles from Beaver) to start our life. Our first child, a daughter, was born there. When I got married, I immediately became active in the Church again. I had gone inactive for a while, but I always knew the Church was right. I always knew that was where I was supposed to be and what I was supposed to do.

I became very involved in Relief Society, and I just loved it. I was one of the few young sisters who loved Relief Society. I learned how to read music, and I got started leading music in Primary and Relief Society. Music followed me everywhere I went.

You hear about some wives falling in love with their husband's family. I fell in love with Stephen, of course, but I also loved his mom as soon as I met her. She was a kind, wise and spiritual lady. She always said there was some special purpose in her son coming home from Vietnam. He was drafted into the Army, and became a forward observer. The job carried a high mortality rate. But my husband was one of the fortunate ones who came back.

But Stephen was not active in the Church. I began praying, asking that my husband become active. For a while he'd attend church, but then he would stop going. Still, I always believed he would eventually come back.

We moved to Arizona for about a year, and that was both a high and low point for us. I had my second child, and Stephen started going to church, but then he had a falling out with our bishop. Later the bishop called me in for an interview. He told me that someone would eventually come along who would activate my husband. I clung to that promise and the faith of that bishop.

When your new baby is only six months old, you usually don't want to have another for a while. But I felt a strong impression, a real yearning to be pregnant again. So we went ahead and conceived. At the same time, I thought, *Whoa, what am I doing?*

There were problems almost immediately. I started getting really sick every six weeks. When I was about four months along, we moved to Houston. I continued getting sick—every six weeks it seemed—with these horrible colds. The baby didn't seem very active in the womb, didn't move a whole lot. Back then we didn't have technology like ultrasound, so I'd go to the doctor and just do the normal monthly routine.

Michael was born six weeks early. My husband said there was a strong feeling—a spirit—in the room as Michael was born. He felt the same strong spirit before, when he was baptized. So Michael was here, and we thought he was okay. I took him home, but about a week later he started throwing up. He'd go purple, then become very pale, and he was just never the same as my other two children. He was listless and never seemed very alert.

At the time, Houston was having floods. I tried to take Michael to the doctor but had to turn back as the streets were flooded. Stephen was stuck out on the freeway for several hours and didn't get home until the early morning. So it was the next day before we could go to see the doctor, who upon seeing Michael immediately sent us to a specialist. All of a sudden that day became one long day of the unknown. We went to the Texas Children's Hospital in downtown Houston. A pediatrician took x-rays of Michael's heart. He decided Michael needed to be seen by cardiologists. My husband had gone home to gather some things and check on our other two children, who we'd left with a friend. By the time he returned, our little boy was in the Intensive Care Unit.

That evening Michael started having convulsions. The next day they gave us the grave news that he had a hypoplastic left heart—the left chamber of his heart was underdeveloped. They decided to operate to see if the right chamber could do both jobs of the heart. But he was just too little and not strong enough to come off the heart pump. He was in the hospital ten days before he died. We took him back to Utah to be buried.

Through all this time my faith never wavered. I remembered something I had learned in Seminary about infants going directly back to our Heavenly Father. I knew Michael needed to be born. He just needed to come and get his body. I also believe it was part of Michael's mission to help my husband. At that time we had a special bishop who befriended Stephen, and that's when he became active in the Church. Since then he has served in many callings, including bishop.

I miss Michael and think of him every day. He is very much a part of our lives, even though he is not with us. It's as though the children we've had since him all bring a small memory of Michael with them, as if they knew him before and know him here.

Michael was going to be our last until we lost him. My husband and I had a talk. I told him I felt we were not done having kids. I immediately wanted to try to have another baby, not to replace Michael, but to fill the void. Yet for some reason, I couldn't get pregnant. A friend of mine had just had her first child. She and her husband had been trying to conceive for ten years before going through the temple. She said to me, "You're not going to have another baby until you guys go to the temple." So in 1976 we went to the temple and were sealed to each other and had little Michael and our two other children sealed to us. And I'll be darned, our second daughter was born almost exactly nine months after that. It was amazing. She just had to be born in the covenant.[4]

That experience gave me a new realization of motherhood—of how important it is. Heavenly Father's spirit children need bodies, and I was willing to have them come down to our home if the Lord trusted me enough to try and bring them up in the gospel. Thus, we've had an even dozen. I have to add, they're cheaper by the dozen, since our last one was free from the hospital!

When one of my twins, Whitney, was seven, she contracted a virus called Transverse myelitis. She was paralyzed from the chest down. Your life

---

4. A child born to a couple sealed under the covenant of eternal marriage in an LDS temple is said to be "born in the covenant."

changes so drastically when your perfect child looses her legs. She has had to live in a wheelchair, and it has been a test of faith for our family. I never questioned why, but I learned what needed to be done to take care of her needs. She has taught me so much of courage and strength. Her twin sister has been a great example of service, as she has been her legs in so many ways.

~

I had a falling out with my foster mother—she wasn't too happy with me getting married. She would have kept all her children from getting married if she could. So I had a falling out with my foster family for a few years. It was then that I started searching for my birth father. I figured he still reported to Immigration, so I started writing to him in care of the Immigration and Naturalization Service, hoping they would forward my letters to him.

One day I got a letter from my natural mother. She wrote to me like we had never skipped a beat, like we had just seen each other last week. Apparently, my father had sent my letters on to her—I didn't even know they had separated. I guess he thought I wanted to be in contact with her. It was an interesting letter. She told me I had a younger brother and two younger half-brothers. Her English was almost perfect. After her death I learned that she dictated her letters to her brother.

I called her that evening, but I never had an urge to go see her. She gave me my natural father's address and phone number, and I called him. They both had strong Chinese accents and broken English, so sometimes it was hard to communicate on the phone, but we would talk. And from that point on, my father would always mail birthday cards and letters to my children, and when I would have a baby. I always felt a real special love for him. I think he would have kept me if I had not been a girl. My natural mother gave him my brother to raise. She never hung onto her children very long.

I learned what little bit I could about our family. My mother told me about an older half-brother. She had been married before she had me, and my half-brother had been killed in a car accident. But I could never get much information from her, and she would not allow me to contact my aunts and uncles. After her death, I learned that I had another half-brother and an older half-sister. They were the siblings of the son who had been killed. The other brother was also in the accident and has permanent brain damage. I keep in touch with my half-sister and found that we have quite a bit in common.

My father passed away before I ever got to go see him. I would write and call, but my brother never told me how sick he was. Perhaps he didn't really know. I had planned on getting over to California one day and seeing him, but with all the children I just never got there. When my brother did realize that he was dying, he let us know. My husband and I tried to get there, but he died while we were en route.

Meeting my brother and my father's people for the first time was strange. I felt really out of place. I looked like them, but I didn't act like them and didn't talk like them. They were all first generation from China. No one spoke English, except Uncle Albert—he's actually a second cousin, but he calls himself my Uncle Albert. The meeting was strange for all of them, too, because I look exactly like my dad. None of them had ever seen me before. It kind of haunted people, I could see.

I didn't feel abandoned by my parents when I was younger, but I felt it as I became a mother. I realized my mom threw me away. She just plain didn't want me. I began to visit with my brother and he would say, "If anything, I would have liked to have been a family. I would've loved to have you as my big sister and pulled your hair." There are times when I've felt bitterness and times I've felt sorry for myself. Yet when I'd get angry, I always felt peace and knew Heavenly Father was there to comfort me. I realized that I can't blame anybody for how I am. I can rise above any circumstance, in spite of how I was raised or the abandonment I felt.

I believe that I have forgiven my foster father for his abuse. I was able to write to him several times and share pictures of my family. He passed on a few years ago, and I hope that he was at peace. Working toward forgiving is hard, but it is always a better journey than holding on to bitterness and anger.

~

There was a point when I lived in Houston, and it seemed that I was surrounded by sisters at church who all had college educations. When we went back to Utah, I finally got my high school diploma. It was good for me to do that. But before that I felt, *Gee, I'm really dumb. I've got all these college ladies around me.* I had a restless feeling, never like I was missing out, but like I wasn't very smart.

Being around these educated women made me realize that I was where I should be in life. I knew I was doing what I was supposed to do, and that was raising my children in a good home. After that realization, I never had a problem. *So what? So they went to college,* I thought. *I'll do that when I want, if I want.* I did well in school when I worked hard, but I just wasn't scholastically inclined. When I finished high school, motherhood was the most important thing.

Education was one matter, but I already had enough hang-ups over being Oriental. One thing that always gets to me is when people ask, "What nationality are you?" Do they ask *you* what nationality you are? I laugh it off, and for the most part I say I'm Chinese, but I've never really liked to acknowledge it because I'm so American. My friends laugh when I say, "Yeah, I'm as American as you are, until I look in the mirror!"

Times have changed from when I was growing up. People are now more accepting of other cultures. Now you can be yourself and be proud of where you come from. I didn't have that. I wasn't taught that being Chinese was okay. I know my foster family thought I was their China doll, but they didn't stop to realize the cultural difference between white and Oriental. They just didn't even see it. But there is something happening in this day and age. It's a more enlightened world, one world, and the gospel helps bring that about.

When my oldest daughter began school, she excelled in all her classes. She was an A student, smart and well-liked. Once, she was ill and missed a day-and-a-half of school. When she came back, every one of those kids stood up and clapped their hands. It felt so good to me because those kids had parents who were my peers, who were my age, and who had once made me feel so bad. It was their children who were cheering, that were so excited to see my daughter. It did my heart good.

Perhaps my children have had slurs said to them. It hurts them and hurts me still, but they always knew that my husband and I were there for them. They knew we would address the situation if need be, but we would let them try to handle it first. We've always tried to help them have confidence in themselves and assure them they are handsome and beautiful, which they are!

We are all, whether in or out of the Church, unique and loved by the Lord. I am grateful, for he has truly blessed my life and has always been there as I prayed. Life is challenging, no matter who you are. Just because we've lived one way, that doesn't mean it's the way we have to live. As I always say, you can rise above circumstances.

You can.

Interview by James Kimball and Kent Miles
May 1, 1997
BYU Women's Conference, Provo, Utah

Telephone interview by Edward Kimball
September 8, 2008

LAUREL THATCHER ULRICH *is a professor of history at Harvard. In 1991 she received the Pulitzer Prize in history for* A Midwife's Tale, *which examines life for ordinary women in the early American republic. It was later developed into a documentary film for the PBS series* The American Experience. *She coined the phrase "Well-behaved women seldom make history," which has become ubiquitous, making its way onto t-shirts, greeting cards, mugs and bumper stickers.*

Laurel Thatcher Ulrich

Historian
Cambridge, Massachusetts

Sugar City, Idaho, was lively for a tiny little town of nine hundred people when I grew up there. It's five miles north of Rexburg along the highway toward Yellowstone. The whole town washed away in the Teton Flood of 1976. By then, my parents had moved to Idaho Falls, but we went back that year to visit. There were two or three buildings still standing that I could remember. Even trees were washed away.

It's an interesting feeling having the material remains of your childhood washed away. Not that there was a lot there anyway, because it was a new town in 1906. It was a sugar factory town. Now it's like a subdivision bedroom community of Rexburg.

This is a Mormon life story because it begins with ancestors. My grandparents had homesteaded in Teton City, near Sugar City, and that's where my mom was born. My dad was also born in Idaho, in the little town of Thatcher. So both of my parents grew up in the age of cattle and sheep, and both of them had sheep, if I'm not mistaken. Dad was a school teacher. The only job he could get was in Teton, and he came out and boarded with my mother's parents. That's how they met. My parents spent almost all of their married life in southeastern Idaho.

We used to say Sugar City was 99.44 percent Mormon. And it really was a very intact and very active Mormon town. Whereas Teton, where my mother grew up, was a backsliding Mormon town, and my mother's family, the Sidoways, were among the backsliders. That was a great dynamic to grow up with. I had Thatcher relatives who were active in the Church and Sidoways who weren't.

My mother was the only one in her family who was active, even though she wasn't baptized until she was sixteen. Her father was never a member of the Church, although his parents had been among the handcart pioneers. There had been disaffection in polygamy times and my grandfather had never been baptized. So my mom had to take a courageous step when she was in her teens to join the Church.

I grew up with a complex understanding of Mormonism because of all of these interesting relatives, all of whom we observed and compared and contrasted and loved. Simultaneously, there was a spirit of strong commitment to the Church and tolerance and love for people who weren't active.

I'm really grateful for that heritage. I grew up prepared to live in a world where not everybody was Mormon.

Because my dad was a teacher and school superintendant, there was always a strong emphasis on learning in our house. My older brothers were examples to me. I can remember going to visit Gordon, who went to law school in Washington, D.C., and Conley, who was in the Air Force. I was in high school and my parents, my sister, and I drove across country to visit them. I remember loving the experience of seeing other parts of the world. So my brothers gave me the example—which my parents probably later regretted—of escaping our tiny little town through books and magazines and the emphasis on education.

As I look back at high school I have some very happy memories. It was a little school, and you could do everything—music, drama, pep club, school newspaper, and all that. Girls weren't encouraged in sports, but you could do almost anything because it was a small school. But it was hard to be intellectually inclined. That's hard anyway in high school—particularly hard, I think, in a small town—and I always felt a little strange.

I'm a maverick in my family in that I didn't do my undergraduate studies at Ricks College.[1] It would have been total abandonment of our region to go to Brigham Young University. Nobody wanted to hear anything about BYU in that part of Idaho—Ricks was the church school. My

---

1. LDS Church–owned university in Rexburg, Idaho; founded in 1888, renamed BYU-Idaho in 2001.

mother had gone to Ricks and my siblings went to Ricks, but I had gotten a scholarship, a national scholarship. My dad just got an idea one day. Something came across his desk about scholarships and SATs. In those years, they didn't give the SAT or ACT at our high school. My dad thought, *Oh, why not?* He was always very proud of us. "Why don't you take this exam, and maybe you could get a scholarship?" They had to set it up especially for me. I was the only kid in Madison County who took the SAT that year.

So I had a national scholarship. It wasn't a lot of money, but the telegram came at noon one day and said I had won this General Motors scholarship. It asked me to list my first-choice school. I hadn't really thought about that. Gordon was at George Washington and that seemed like a long way away. I thought, *Gosh, I can go someplace other than Ricks?* By then my other brother was out of the military and at the University of Utah. My grandparents still lived in Salt Lake so we just wired back, "University of Utah." That's about as much thought as I gave it.

It was an exciting experience to be at the University of Utah. I had a great time. I felt anonymous—which was really nice after being the superintendent's daughter in a little town—and also challenged. I had friends from all over the country. All of the out-of-state students, and there weren't that many, were lumped together. My roommate was a ballet dancer from California. I was a debater and the debate team got me acquainted with lots of fun, lively people. Eventually I found my way to the English department.

I received a very good education at the U., but my assumption was that I would get married and have children. After that, I didn't know what else. I was perfectly happy. I seemed to enjoy doing anything. I was active in the LDS Institute of Religion and had the wonderful influence of Lowell Bennion[2] and T. Edgar Lyon.[3] I had a rich, challenging, expansive, humane kind of religious education, as well as a great academic education. And good friends, of course. I met my husband, Gael, there and we were married while still in school.

If you were to ask, "How do you go from being a small-town Mormon girl to being a professor?" I would say that a common theme in my life has been support from the men I know. My father was a great booster of all his children. He was really wonderful that way, and as a teacher I don't think he differentiated between us in any way. He may have in other areas, but not academically. We were encouraged to be serious about school.

The second man in my life, of course, would be my husband Gael. When we were married there was never a thought that I would quit school. The way we saw it, I had a scholarship, I should use it. We didn't think beyond a bachelor's, but that was the primary goal, that I finish that degree.

In the 1950s we just didn't think about any conflict between educa-tion and motherhood. There was no conflict because there were so few

---

2. Lowell L. Bennion (1908–1996), an educator who was the founding director of the LDS Institute of Religion, adjacent to the University of Utah. He is known for his practical theology and humanitarian work, such as Utah's first food bank.

3. T. Edgar Lyon (1903–1978), an eminent LDS historian and educator.

opportunities for women. I remember going to see the dean of women, who talked about women and careers. None of us knew what she was talking about. I felt like it was a tremendous achievement just to graduate from college. My goal was never a career. It was to finish school, and I didn't really think much beyond that.

Gael graduated a year ahead of me. He had some opportunities for graduate school and jobs, but decided to stay at the U. another year and do his masters so that it wouldn't disrupt my education. That was a really fateful decision.

⌒

After I graduated, we moved to Massachusetts and our first child, Karl, was born. Gael was doing his Ph.D. in chemical engineering at MIT. We lived there through the '60s, and in a way it was my second education. Even though I was never in a classroom, living in Boston was my graduate school—being part of the LDS community, with the civil rights movement taking off and being involved in that in a modest way.

One experience that was important in terms of my development as a writer was editing a Church-sponsored guidebook called A Beginner's Boston. That would have been '65 or '66. Our bishop thought the ward should write a guidebook for newcomers to Boston. There was a continual flow of students and other newcomers, and the Cambridge Ward was always organized to orient people.

This is a wonderful story, and I'm sure it's been embellished over the years. We presented the idea to the elders quorum,[4] which was filled with students at the business school. The quorum said, "Oh, this would never work. It's a bad idea." So then we presented it to the Relief Society, who said, "That's a great idea. We'll do it!"

So the guidebook became a Relief Society project. To design the layout, we used a refrigerator drawer with a glass top, and put a little light inside to make an illuminated table. We created this little guidebook, which sold out before we even had all the copies from the printer. Our Relief Society president had decided to call the *Boston Globe* to see if they'd interview us. They were so impressed that they wrote glowing things about it. It was quite a clever little guide and there was nothing else like it. Even though we didn't have any experience with this sort of thing, it looked professional because all these smart people worked on it.

By that time I realized that there was life after marriage. Although I loved doing things in the Church, I always tended toward overkill. I would throw myself wholeheartedly into any project. At some point you realize all your energy is not going to fit into that little package of teaching once a month in Relief Society. I think that's happened to lots of women.

The guidebook was an extremely important moment for me. We were just getting started out. I had these little kids and not much money. It

---

4. Generally, most of the adult males in a ward (or congregation).

occurred to me that I could do a lot with small amounts of time if I was organized. It was very hard at first, but I became disciplined. The whole experience convinced me that I could handle taking a class or two, and eventually I started thinking about the long term.

So Gael and I came up with the money for me to take one course. We thought that if I got a masters in English, at some point I could teach part-time. That seemed like it would be a nice outlet while my kids were growing up. It was a one-year masters program that took five years for me to do.

Now, an important point here: in the early '60s, the women's movement was gradually starting. In 1963, I read Betty Friedan's *The Feminine Mystique,* and I think that had a lot to do with my direction. The way I read it was maybe not the way everyone read it, but I read it as saying, "You have a long life and you need to have a 'life plan.'" I think that idea is in there. So getting this part-time masters was my life plan toward sometime in the indeterminate future when I might not be totally engaged with my children.

By the late '60s, there really was a feminist movement taking off, and it was getting national press. At that point Claudia Bushman[5] said to me, "I'm going to do something nobody's done before. I'm going to study women's history." I thought, *Boy, that's unusual!* All my stuff was the standard curriculum for masters in literature, which meant almost all male writers and nothing very unusual. Then another friend who was teaching in the area started to

---

5. Claudia Bushman (1934-), professor of American Studies at Columbia University.

read a lot of feminist literature and she knew a lot of women who were interested in these ideas. We decided we ought to get together and see if this had anything to do with us.

We started meeting as a group in the summer of 1970. Around that time, Gene England[6] came through on a visit to the Bushmans. Claudia was telling him about what we were doing and he said, "Why don't you do an issue of *Dialogue?*"[7]

Many of the women in this group had been involved in *A Beginner's Guide to Boston* and we were used to doing these collective projects. We thought, *Why not? We'll edit an issue of* Dialogue. It didn't seem like a big deal because everybody in the Cambridge Ward read *Dialogue* anyway. We weren't in any hostile environment. And so we did it. That's the famous "Pink Issue" of *Dialogue* (summer 1971).

When I moved to New Hampshire the next year, I continued to come back to Boston about once a month as we were completing the *Dialogue* issue. By then the LDS Institute of Religion in Cambridge had organized to give a course: "Pioneer Mormon Women." That became the book *Mormon Sisters: Women in Early Utah,* which Claudia Bushman edited. I contributed a little essay on literature.

---

6. Eugene England (1933–2001), founding editor of *Dialogue*, critic, essayist, teacher, and pioneering scholar in the field of Mormon letters.

7. *Dialogue: A Journal of Mormon Thought*, an independent quarterly established to express Mormon culture and to examine the relevance of religion to secular life.

I tell my students who have forgotten or never knew, that there was a time when people expected women to sit back and retire from life once they got married; that it wasn't a natural progression to go through marriage and raise children and come out the other end with an academic career. There was a women's movement that made that possible, in which groups of women worked together to create something collectively.

⁓

Gael and I always had a great partnership, but it had been pretty traditional in the way we divided things. In thinking through all of this, it became clear that there were lots of ways to live your life. Gael went into teaching because he was disaffected with the commuter life, working for a corporation where he was going to do less and less research and more and more administration. He liked being in the lab. The fact that he went into teaching gave us flexibility that soon allowed me to start doing more graduate work.

There was no way we could have handled our kids and the Church and his job and me in school if I had commuted to Boston. So I studied history part-time at the University of New Hampshire. It was a small state university and I was a faculty wife, which got me a tuition break (I think it was half). Still, it was more expensive than in the West. We lived within walking distance of the university, so Gael could run home while I went to class. I got my B.A. in English in 1960, an M.A. in English in 1971, and my Ph.D. in history in 1980. During those years, Gael and I raised five children—Karl, Melinda, Nathan, Thatcher and Amy.

When I look back and think of our life, I realize we were kind of crazy. We never were into furniture and vacations and cars, but we were always into making things. Gael built our house with his hands. He put all his spare time into carpentry and I put my time into writing. The kids are amazingly creative, but they were deprived because they never got to watch much television. Their spouses tell them they're out of it.

I absolutely adore learning and have always felt comfortable doing it, not that it isn't hard work. But because I loved it so, I was happy to get up at five in the morning in order to write. When I was writing my dissertation and all my kids were in school, I would get up at 5:00 and write until 7:00, when I needed to get everybody up to go to school. And I would just be a crab. It would be like murder to come down and get their lunches ready and get them out the door. By then I was shot and I couldn't go back to writing.

So we worked out this deal. We figured out that Gael was perfectly capable of making breakfast and getting them out to school. That seems like such a simple thing now. We laugh about it, but it was hard. I'd be upstairs working and I could hear everything that was going on downstairs. I would want to intervene and organize and do it my way. "You're going to miss the bus if you don't do such-and-such." And he'd let them miss the bus, which was good for them because then they had to be accountable. He got extremely creative in the way he did breakfast. It was really a wonderful thing. It meant I could work from five in the morning until 11:30, and I didn't want to write any longer than that.

We always had a joke in our family about the high school kid whose mother still wrote his name on his lunch with magic markers every morning. My kids made their own lunches and did their own laundry as soon as they could press the button to open the washing machine. They had to. And they are just terrific people. They can do anything.

They're good kids and have succeeded in part because I wasn't a stereotypically good mom. It's kind of ironic. If I had known that when I was younger, I'd have been much more peaceful about my life.

⁓

Our older children are all about two years apart. At one point we had three kids in college all at once. By the time Karl went on a mission we were in that horrible financial crunch. I was through with my degrees and had started to work and bring in some income, every penny of which went to tuition. In the end, it was enough to get by. We didn't plan it, but it worked.

At first I had an adjunct position at the University of New Hampshire in the humanities program. I did that for about four years. By then my first book was published.[8] I had a fellowship with the National Endowment for the Humanities to write, and one of my mentors left the university. That meant the school had a position in my field. There was a wonderful depart-

---

8. *Good Wives: Images and Reality in the Lives of Women in Northern New England, 1650–1750* (Alfred A. Knopf, 1982).

ment chair who stuck his neck out and redefined the position somewhat so that it looked like me. They did a national search, but I was well qualified because the position was more or less written for me.

So then I went into a full-time faculty position. That was 1985, so I was pretty old. You can do the math. I was born in 1938, and I didn't have a full-time job until I was forty-seven. Actually, I had lots of full-time jobs, but I wasn't paid.

My second book, A Midwife's Tale,[9] which was published in 1990, truly changed my life. The years since then have been unbelievable, really. I won the Pulitzer Prize for that book in 1991. I had applied for a Guggenheim Fellowship the year before, just after my book came out, and there was a blank in the application that said "Awards." I remember typing, "None." And in the next year I had almost every award that you could get for that one book, which is sort of bizarre.

The year after the Pulitzer, I came West and gave talks at the University of Utah, BYU, Ricks College and my high school. I came home from Salt Lake and went into my office and there was a little pink slip of paper saying, "Call the MacArthur Foundation at this number." I thought, *Oh, they must want a letter of recommendation for someone.* Twenty minutes later the phone rang and it was the *Boston Globe* saying, "We want to know

9. *A Midwife's Tale: The Life of Martha Ballard, Based on Her Diary, 1785–1812* (Vintage Books, 1991).

how it felt to win the MacArthur Award." I said, "What? I don't know anything about that! I guess I'd better return this phone call."

The size of the MacArthur grant is dependent on your age, which was one of the really wonderful things about being older. And you get it no matter what you do. You can bank it, you can give it away, you can invest it in the stock market. They don't want a report, they just give you the money. It's very strange. But it's an opportunity to do what you want to do.

I didn't really know how to deal with it. I've done all my work around the margins of responsibility. I'm a five-in-the-morning person, I'm the one who has to get it done before the next obligation comes up. I've learned to be responsive to everybody else's needs and to feel like my own work was a special gift that came when I could afford it. For someone to say, "Here is the money to do as you please," was an extremely disorienting experience, which I still haven't totally come to terms with.

When the MacArthur fellowship was awarded I was totally exhausted. I hardly knew who I was because I'd had so much adulation. With the adulation came a whole new set of obligations: come and speak here, come and be this role model, come and exemplify this, come and speak to the nurses, come and talk to the midwives, come and talk to these poor continuing education students, come and raise money for the university. And foolishly—I think my Mormon upbringing conduces this—you do what you're called to do. So I was running around doing all this stuff, trying to be very accessible.

I'd say the MacArthur rescued me from my own success. It did two things for me. Number one: it said, "Your time is valuable." Number two: boy, it made life easier. If I needed something like a computer, I could just go get it. I could employ my students as assistants. I could say to them, "Don't worry, you've got summer support." It's been a joy to be able to employ these wonderful, struggling students.

I've been working with a young filmmaker on a documentary film of *A Midwife's Tale* for PBS. I was able to work closely with her and learn a lot about the world of film. But I couldn't have done it without the MacArthur buying away some of my teaching time at UNH.

The Harvard professorship was an unexpected opportunity. I didn't anticipate teaching here, but I am now in my second year, and I love it. Accepting Harvard's offer was the right thing to do, even though some people warned me against it. Harvard has not had a very good reputation for its treatment of women. Fortunately, that is changing, though with so few senior women on the faculty, the burdens are sometimes overwhelming. I'm going to take some time off next year to finish my next book.[10]

~

The notion of a world in which men earn a living and women stay at

---

10. *The Age of Homespun: Objects and Stories in the Creation of an American Myth.* (Alfred A. Knopf, 2001).

home and nurture a family can account for probably less than two percent of human history, if that. It's a particular artifact of a particular kind of capitalistic economy that came about in the 1950s. That was an anomalous time in human history. I think of my own mother. She never "worked" outside the home, but she canned tons of food, made all the clothes—and what did it take to do laundry in those days? When I think of the kind of work that it took just to get food on the table and clothes on kids' backs, it required incredible physical labor. That work was done in the home and that has been true from time immemorial.

Women have *always* worked. I just can't say that loud enough and long enough. What's happened since World War II is that the economy has increasingly taken work out of the homes. There's nothing that can put it back, it's been taken out of the home unless you happen to live on a farm. Even then I don't think there are many of those little farms or small towns left. You can't afford to sew your own children's clothing now because of the price of fabric. The economy has shifted so that it's a complex world economy, and in order to survive people have to be in the wage economy. I think that's sad. I wish there were more ways we could subvert that and work against it.

What I'm trying to say to some of our leaders is that we have to find a way to preserve the values of Mormon culture in a capitalist society. You cannot put a population consisting of women with children into a time warp and freeze them and say, "We're going to be holdouts against social change." If you do that, (A) the institutional church is going to lose women because it doesn't conform to the reality of their lives; and (B) it will create a lot of crazy people who are trying to figure out how to hold this thing together.

What I would like to hear more of from the Church is: children matter. All children matter. The children of the poor matter, the children of the rich matter, middle-class children matter. What can we do as Latter-day Saints to provide for our children the best possible environment at home, and in school and in church and in the economy? How can we take care of them? There has to be some collective effort to do that. It can't be done individually, house by house. We have to find some way to do that.

My experience in the Cambridge Ward with women collectively working to solve problems was really wonderful. It was done on a voluntary basis. It would be good if we could, in some way, get behind social efforts to make life better for everybody's children. Now I'm sounding like the daughter of a school superintendent, but I really do think we've got to have good teachers for schools. In order to have good teachers for schools, good nurses in hospitals, executives who are humane, you've got to break down this notion that men are out there running the world and women are going to pick up all the pieces with no resources and no social capital behind them.

And so I say to women, go out and change the world. Whether you're seven or seventy, there's work out there to be done, go to it! But you have to be educated. If we listen to our general Relief Society presidency[11]

---

11. Elaine Jack, Chieko Okazaki and Aileen H. Clyde served in the general Relief Society presidency from 1990 to 1997.

and do what they're saying, we'll be in great shape. I would love to hear less about roles and where we're supposed to be and what we're supposed to be doing. It's more about values and spirituality and what it means to be a Christian, and how we can live the gospel in whatever setting we may find ourselves. That's what I'm hearing from our general Relief Society presidency, and I think it's fascinating.

Our greatest gift, what is special about Latter-day Saints, is not necessarily our ability to raise families. Lots of people do that pretty well, and frankly, sometimes we don't do it so well. Our greatest gift is our ability to create communities out of people who have nothing in common. We learn to be brothers and sisters and take care of each other and live together. I really believe in that, and it's what I want to preach to the world—how to make us more engaged and involved. It isn't the only place, but I think the Church is a great learning arena for many other settings out there in the world, and if we try to apply our religion we can make a difference by having a vision of community.

Much of that vision for the Church is really my vision for the world, and it's a lot of what I try to understand in my scholarship: How do ordinary people put a life together and deal with their adversities and trials? I don't go looking for Mormon answers, but in my questions something can be drawn from the gospel. And you can distinguish between the Church and the gospel, too. In my experience, the Church has been a training ground for all kinds of things, including values. The gospel, on the other hand, says that we are children of God and life has a purpose and we have a destiny, that there is a reality beyond this moment and this life. I always wish I were a better example of those things.

Interview by James Kimball and Kent Miles
February 3, 1997
Cambridge, Massachusetts

CATHERINE M. STOKES *is a professional nurse who has held a variety of positions in health care in Illinois, including bedside nursing, office nursing, public health regulation and bioterrorism preparedness and response. She retired after thirty-four years of service in the Illinois Department of Public Health and now resides in Salt Lake City.*

Catherine M. Stokes

Public Health Administrator
Salt Lake City, Utah

I was born in rural Mississippi. My family was a sharecropping family, farming someone else's land and paying the rent with a portion of the crop. We had very little. It was a joke that the Depression came and went in my town and nobody noticed. It was that poor. There were five children living at that time, and I am the youngest of those five. Two of us survive now.

For a variety of reasons, it was decided that I would be given to a great-aunt to be raised, and so she came out to the country to get me. I was about four years old, as much as I can remember and piece together. I recall they came in a car, and I left there in a little flour sack dress.

We went to New Orleans where her husband had relatives. When we arrived, they were having dinner. They had fried fish and spaghetti, and they put it on a plate. I had never eaten on a plate before. In Mississippi, we would get our food on those little tin pie pans, and you'd take your food, find a place on the floor to sit, and eat it with your fingers. Nobody in the house had read Emily Post. So I took this plate, and the feel of it was different, and I went to sit on the floor. My great-aunt, who is now my mother, reached down and took my arm and said, very gently, "We don't do that any more." So for the first time, I sat at a table and tried to maneuver using a utensil. The next day, the three of us boarded the train for Chicago as a new family.

I was now growing up in Chicago with my new mother and father, who themselves had no formal education. I am convinced they taught themselves to read and write. She worked as a domestic; he was a bricklayer. I do not know how he learned that trade, but he was very skilled. He could lay a thousand bricks a day.

Unlike my home in Mississippi, I had enough of everything living with them. I had enough food to eat and I had clothes to wear. I was told that I had to study hard to get an education, and that I had to get the highest marks in school—that was my job. As I think about that, I realize that Heavenly Father sent me here with the gift of not knowing there are things you might not be able to do, and so I did everything I was told to do. I had no idea how deprived we were. I didn't realize that until I had gone to college, and then I thought, *Wow, I probably should have ended up a criminal!* But there is good in everything, and this time there was good in not knowing.

My parents sent me to a Catholic school because the Catholic schools were the best in Chicago. I was expelled because I challenged a nun who said that anybody who wasn't Catholic was going to Hell. I said, "No, we're not Catholic, and we're not going to Hell." I went home in fear and trepidation, thinking I was going to get it, but my folks just put me in another school.

I was feisty, if the same person can be feisty and submissive. Somehow, I have always known I am a child of God. I may have not known it in those words, but I always knew that I'm loved, I'm powerful, and I'm good. I don't know where that knowledge came from, and so I say that it was a gift, a gift that I was given to make this journey with.

My mother knew that Hyde Park High School was one of the best public schools in the city. She went over to that neighborhood and asked another woman, a black woman, if we could use her address so I could go to the best high school in the city. And so I went to Hyde Park. I did very well in high school because I was supposed to. Mother told me, "That's your job."

My parents did the best they could with what they had, living on the upper edge of poverty. They had an abundance of what people in the country call "mother wit"—a common sense kind of thing. They observed the people around them. Mother worked for wealthy people and she noticed how they raised their kids. She used a lot of what she learned in raising me.

I graduated from high school in 1954. Chicago is a racially segregated city, often described as the most segregated in America. Our class was probably ninety-seven percent Jewish. There was a set of Japanese twins who told us stories of their lives in the concentration camps during World War II. There was a sprinkling of blacks, including me.

I had the honor of being named the outstanding senior of my graduating class—quite an accomplishment. When I went to get my picture taken for *The Chicago Tribune*'s neighborhood section, I was so proud, I can't even describe it to you. When I got off the bus and began walking toward the Tribune Tower, a pigeon deposited all his day's food on my head. You can't imagine how I felt! Because of the way we wore our hair back then (it was a real involved process and it had to be washed and straightened) this was a disastrous situation. Fortunately, there was a white reporter who understood how to handle black hair, and she got it cleaned out and the picture was fine. Now, every time I need a little teaspoon of reality, when I'm a little heady, I think about that pigeon and I give thanks for him. But I hope never to meet him or his descendants again!

One of the great hurts in my life occurred in high school, with a girl I had been good friends with. We swapped lunches, exchanged secrets, whatever. I was downtown on a Saturday when I saw this girl walking toward me with a group of her friends. She didn't say hello. She looked right through me. I decided then that would never happen to me again.

I had a hard time in nursing school. There was extra pressure on black students. You had to do more to get less. At this particular school, there was a quota of three black students for each entering class. I was the fourth. I had only been accepted because my high school teacher wanted me to go to this school. I found out years later that her brother was the chairman of the board of the entity that owned the school. So I had an extra measure of pressure because I wasn't supposed to be there.

I loved caring for patients, but I had had several encounters with an instructor. I threw a tray of medications at her because she had been on my back, and I was tired of it. Afterwards, I went up to my room and started packing.

I was called to the office. The incident frightened the faculty because here was a black child who has this much anger simmering just below the surface. They just knew I was crazy, so they sent me to the psychiatrist. He was a kind man who asked me if I wanted to stay in school. I told him, "Yes, but not if I have to kiss somebody's ass to do it." He said, "Well, you don't have to do that, but you do have to come see me for a few weeks. Bring some books to read or do your homework, and sometimes we'll chat." And he did talk with me. I walked away from that experience knowing that you have to learn how to express anger in acceptable ways. Throwing trays at instructors was not an acceptable way.

When I finished nursing school, the director of the school said to me, "Miss Moore, there were times when we did not believe you would make it through this program, not because of your grades, but because of your attitude." I just smiled because I had my diploma by then.

When I was twenty-five, I met the man who would become my husband. I married him because I thought it was time to get married. My friends were married, and I wanted to have a family. But I had no real concept of family. I surely did not have "the ideal family life," whatever that is. And so I married a bright, handsome, charming man on Valentine's Day in 1960. I was kind of a romantic—I still am.

I gave birth to twin boys that December. They were premature and did not live. Two years later, my daughter, Ardelia Kay, was born. Unfortunately, my husband and I hadn't talked through things like what we believed in. We discovered that we had some real different views about how a marriage should work. Shortly after my daughter was born, the marriage abruptly ended.

We always hear about taking care of the widows. I learned that there was a great difference in the way people treated widows and divorced women. So I would say I was a widow, that my husband's departure was sudden and unexpected, and people would be very kind to me. But in the rest of the world it wasn't so easy. When I went to renew the lease on my apartment, the landlord didn't want to renew it. He said he needed my husband to sign for the apartment. I thought about it, called him, and said, "Tell you what, take me to court, and I guarantee you I can stay in your house six months for free. So if you'd rather do that than take this rent I have been paying you every month, that's your choice." I signed the lease, sent it back to him, and he took it. That was that. He didn't bother me the next year when the lease came up.

I had charge accounts before I got married and I had switched them to my husband's name after we married. When we separated, I wanted to switch them back but the store wouldn't do that. So I went to the manager's office and reasoned with him that this was *my* account, it had always been paid and being treated like this was grossly unfair. He okayed the account.

Another blessing was that I didn't have a spirit of fear. I remember when my daughter was a young child growing up, she must have been seven or eight, and we lived on a block with gangs. One day my mother called me at work to say that one of the gangs had taken my daughter's bike. I put my stuff down at work, went home, and went down the alley looking for those gang members. I went up and down the alley, using terms I won't repeat, saying that if she couldn't play on this block nobody would. "Bring me that bike!" I yelled.

They did.

So she played safely on the block because the word was passed: "Don't bother that little girl. Her mother is crazy." It was the instinct a mother lion has, and I see it in women, whether it's their child or any child. Not all women want children or necessarily like children, but for those women with that maternal instinct, there is fierceness about protecting children that I believe is a gift from God. We need to nurture it these days.

⁓

In June 1978, I went to Hawaii for the American Nurse's Association Convention. On the plane, the pilot told funny jokes—I know now that he was LDS. As we approached Oahu, he told us we should visit the Polynesian Cultural Center and the LDS temple—that we would not have this opportunity many times in our life. As it turned out, the temple had just been renovated and the Mormons were having an open house.

When we got to the island there was news of a change in policy in the LDS Church about black members holding the priesthood. I didn't know anything about Mormons. I had heard about the Mormon Tabernacle Choir, but I didn't know there was a religion associated with it. So I put the temple down on my little list of places to go.

When we made it over to the temple, we found out the open house had ended the day before. We went to the visitors' center where we heard the Joseph Smith story. We saw a film about the Book of Mormon and when it was over I asked a missionary, "What happened to the gold plates?" My recollection is that he stammered around this, and I thought, *Well, with gold, you probably have them hidden away someplace.* But I signed the little slip asking for more information, expecting to get a magazine and a request for a donation.

Some weeks later my doorbell rang. I asked who it was, and they said, "The elders." I thought, *Elders?* They sounded young and white. I buzzed them into the building, and there were these two nice, young, white boys in shirts and ties. It was after dark and I said, "What in the hell are you all doing out here?" They said, "We're missionaries for The Church of Jesus Christ of Latter-day Saints." I offered them a drink or a cup of coffee or a Coke, and they refused it all. I thought, *Hey, these are weird white folks.* So we started to chat, and they wanted to know if they could come back. And they did. They came back for months. I bet I went through at least six sets of them.

By the first of the year, in '79, they had convinced me to visit the ward. There I saw all these young, thin, beautiful white women, and I thought, *Well, nothing here for me.* But later I realized that I did not disbelieve what these people had been saying. I have to say it that way. I couldn't say I believed, but I didn't *disbelieve.* I started thinking about that, and I realized that at some point I had stopped smoking, and that got my attention. I couldn't figure out why. Subconsciously, did I quit because these kids are coming over and I don't want to offend them?

When you're facing the truth, the ball is in your court and you have to do something about it. So I returned to the ward in more seriousness. While sitting in one of those yellow chairs in the chapel, this precious little girl came over to me and crawled up into my lap. She started playing with my hair. It was longer then, so it would spring back. Her parents turned every shade of red. You could see the red go up her dad's neck and come around the ears. I was tickled by that, because it was obvious that this kid was so innocent.

For me, one of the great appeals of the Church was the correlation between what they said they believed and what they did. These young men convinced me they were serious about it. They didn't drink and they didn't smoke. They believed in faithfulness and celibacy before marriage. I had already come to a testimony of celibacy if you were single. Sex without commitment is empty. That correlation was a great selling point for me.

The fact that the Church was overwhelmingly white didn't bother me. I have often been in situations where I'm the only black person. I was the first black professional to work for any state nurse association and the first black to work for *any* state health-planning agency. So I am accustomed to being in the minority.

I sensed something in these church folks, but it wasn't hostility. I'd catch folks staring at me. Once, I said to a guy, "Why are you staring?" He said, "Well, because I've never known anybody who's black." So then I began inviting people and their families to my home for dinner.

⌒

I love the women of the Church. They have nurtured me; they have taught me; they have been great examples. I've watched the young women in my ward with their children, accomplishing great things. I've watched them teaching and training, doing it to varying degrees, some more skilled than others. I look at other young women in my ward who are studying, who are also accomplishing great things. And there are some who manage to combine both.

I also have concern for the women in the Church because I see some who feel that they are powerless. While I realize that women lack formal power, we are not powerless. When you look at what those pioneer sisters did, when you look at how they came across the plains—when a woman died, her baby was passed off to another woman. They shared whatever they had. When I think of the Relief Society selling wheat to the government during World War I, setting up schools and all that, I wonder, *What happened? How did we get to this place?*

I'm taken back to the importance of knowing who you are. If I believe I am the daughter of the power that created the universe, I have more power than I will ever be able to use. Now, if I believe that, then I act in a certain way. Not in arrogance, but in certainty. If I believe that I came here to be challenged and refined, to grow and develop my talents, then I should be ready to take on any task. You have to know who you are and you have to internalize that. And if you want to know whether you have accomplished that, then look at what it is you're doing with your life. That's the real deal, versus what you say you believe.

I ask young women to remember the words of the Apostle Paul to Timothy: "For God hath not given us a spirit of fear; but of power, and of love, and of a sound mind" (2 Timothy 1:7). If you have a spirit of fear, it didn't come from your Heavenly Father. You need to examine where it may have come from. If you're not in the appropriate frame of mind or if your behavior isn't what you want it to be, then you need to get on your knees and pour out your heart, just as Joseph did in that grove.

I believe one reason black people have survived in this country is because we've been forgiving. Despite the ravages of slavery and the traditions of segregation and discrimination, you have to forgive and move on. We need to ask our Heavenly Father, as individuals and collectively, what we're supposed to be doing and then we need to get on with it. Do not waste your energy being offended. Let it go. When you spend time being offended it saps your energy and your strength. And what good ever came from taking offense? Keep your eye on the prize. In my Chicago neighborhood we say, "Keep your eye on the donut, not the hole."

If we are to get beyond this great racial divide, we're going to have to know more about each other. We're going to have to serve, so we know and love one another. I see it as a circle of serving, knowing and loving. It is incumbent upon us to set an example for the rest of the world, because we are the church of Jesus Christ.

So I say to my brothers and sisters, white and black, "Don't let racism—mine, yours or anybody else's—get in the way of your salvation." Come and see for yourself. Are there racists in the LDS Church? You bet there are. There are racists everywhere. God made so many of them, he must love them. He loves us all. I would rather face a racist in the context of the Church than outside the Church, because then I can call them to repentance in the name of Jesus Christ.

~

In the Church, we seem to have Noah's Ark syndrome, as I call it. Everything is two by two. And yet we are born alone, we are baptized alone, we are confirmed alone, we die alone, and we will stand in judgment alone. While nothing is more blessed than a loving marriage, not all of us are going to have one. God loves us all the same. Look at the numbers, there are not enough men for every woman who wants one.

Marriage can be wonderful, but it isn't the only way to lead a good life. All women are single at some point in their lives. You're single before you marry, and most women outlive their husbands, and they're single again. You can have a wonderful life being single. You can serve. As a matter of fact, you may be in a situation of being freer to serve because you don't have immediate responsibilities for someone else. Don't waste your time feeling sorry for yourself. You agreed to come to this life to have challenging experiences, which may include being single. If you view that as a burden that you're to carry, then carry it gracefully. Even if you know you're going to get married, you should be studying, improving yourself, because we need women with knowledge raising our children. It is the most difficult job you will ever have!

As a community of saints, we need to be examples to the young women coming up. You can lead a virtuous life as a single woman. Sex is not an entitlement. It's not life's bread and water. Marriage is not an entitlement. The Apostle Paul said, "I can do all things through Christ, who strengthens me" (Philippians 4:13). We can do all that we need to do. Stop defining yourself only in relation to somebody else. Be a whole person, first and foremost, a whole daughter of God. Don't think of yourself as a second-class citizen. A wise friend, who has been single all of her life, says that if Heavenly Father needed her to be married, she would be married. So he must want her to be single.

To those young women who think that they're less than men, I remind you that God made Eve to be a help*meet* for Adam—look up the word "helpmeet." When I talk to young women I ask, "Do you think God's as smart as Brigham Young?" Now they usually say, "What's wrong with Sister Stokes?" Remember when Brigham sent out a rescue party to get the saints who were trapped en route in winter? Do you think he called for the sick or the weak to go get them? No, he had to send the strongest to bring them in. You have to be at least as strong as a man to help him.

The single most important decision that I have made in my life was to join The Church of Jesus Christ of Latter-day Saints. The only regret I have is that I didn't come to the Church sooner. I'm grateful that my daughter had the benefit of the gospel in her life at a much earlier age than I did, and that she has many years left to benefit from it.

I have no illusions about the problems in the Church, because *we* are the church and *we* have problems. Though there are pimples and acne on the face of the Church, it still is the best thing that has happened in my life, and there is a place in it for everybody who will come. Let us be knit together in love, that we may come unto Christ and help others to come unto Christ. Let us go about our Father's business together—single, married, male, female, black, white. He invites us all to come unto him. Let none stand in our way.

Interview by James Kimball and Kent Miles
January 17, 1998
Salt Lake City, Utah

TSOBINAR TADEVOSYAN *spent five years in Stalin's Gulag during the 1950s. Her crime was having a brother who protested the forced relocation of native Armenians. He was arrested and shot by the Soviet KGB. Tsobinar and her family were sent to Siberia, where they experienced unimaginable trials and terrors. At the time of this interview, she was visiting Salt Lake City to be baptized. Although she had taught Sunday School classes for years, she wanted to wait and be baptized with her son in Salt Lake, where he and his family had emigrated. Tsobinar passed away in 2006.*

Tsobinar Tadevosyan

Gulag Survivor, Teacher
Yerevan, Armenia

I was born in July 6, 1930, in Tbilisi, Georgia.[1] Both my parents were Armenian. They were survivors of the genocide of 1915 in Turkey.[2] My father was an actor and my mother was a teacher. I had four brothers, but only one survived. His name was Andronik. He was the oldest and he was an actor, too, in Tbilisi.

The Turks killed my grandfather in the genocide. He was a lawyer and they killed him along with most of my father's family. They captured my grandmother and sent

---

1. Georgia was then a Soviet republic on the Black Sea.
2. Beginning in World War I, the Ottoman Empire killed more than one million Armenians.

her to a camp in Turkey. My aunt, with her two children, jumped from the bridge to avoid falling into the hands of the Turks. My other aunt just disappeared.

In Georgia, in 1949, the KGB started arresting Armenian families.[3] They just took whole families and put them in trains on cattle cars. All the intelligent, educated people were being arrested. Then we heard that poets and artists and writers, not to mention many of our teachers, were disappearing. They just disappeared. After a while, we learned that they had been imprisoned. At that time they didn't do anything to our family.

But it was happening all around us—our friends and neighbors, my teachers, all Armenians. And every day, when we'd see someone we knew, we'd give each other hugs and start crying. We were so happy that we were still there, that we had not been sent to prison.

I had not met my husband yet, but on June 14, 1949, the KGB arrested his family. They were arresting whole families and sending them to Siberia. It was not a prison, but the forced relocation of families, thousands of miles from their homes. People were told they would be living in this town in Siberia. Those who resisted were arrested and taken to the KGB building in Tbilisi. There were trials, beatings, killings and disappearances. On June 14, 1949, in just one day they arrested—I don't know how many families— one hundred, two hundred, a thousand. I don't know how many families.

---

3. Under Stalin, several million people of various ethnic backgrounds were relocated or killed in what became known as The Great Purge.

When the KGB started doing this, my family was worried because we were just like those who were disappearing. My brother was really scared. As an Armenian man he was concerned about what was happening all around him, not only to Armenians. They were catching some Georgians, too.

My brother knew that they would eventually arrest him. He said if we didn't do anything, we couldn't change anything. He decided to print brochures warning people to be careful. He denounced what the KGB and the government were doing, crying out that it was not right. He warned that if they continued, the day would come when they would answer to the people for what they did. In the mornings and late at night he would post these brochures on walls around the neighborhood. After that he started going to theaters and cinemas. In the middle of the show he'd throw the brochures from the balcony.

I think he was right in what he was doing. He was one of the few who stood up. There needs to be someone to tell the government that they are not doing right, and he was the one who did that. He knew that they would catch him. He sacrificed himself for the nation, not only for Armenians. Most of the time he was writing not only for Armenians, not only for Georgians, but for all the people of the Soviet Union, for all nationalities.

When my brother was arrested, I was teaching at a school very far from Tbilisi. There were no telephones. I didn't know what was happening to my family. Two days after they had been arrested, the KGB came to my village and arrested me. I was in the middle of my lesson. They just came into my class and took me away.

I arrived in the Gulag on October 12, 1952. It took three days going from Moscow to Siberia—three days without stopping. I was tired and depressed. All my family had been arrested and they received longer sentences than I did. I got ten years in prison and five years probation in the same town, not having any rights. I asked them to please let me say goodbye to my mother. They didn't let me.

Until Stalin's death on March 5, 1953, it was very, very bad. I was stuck in this camp, isolated and separated. There were soldiers standing in towers and guards walking around with dogs . . . lots of dogs. The soldiers looking after us were told that all these women were enemies of the Soviet Union, so they watched us very closely. Most of the time they were laughing at us. They had a prison for men, too, but it was separate.

I was in a building that had two floors filled with bunk beds. We were packed like fish. The room was made for fifteen people, but more than fifty lived there. We had one toilet and sink in the same room. They gave us black wool clothes to wear, and we were taken to the woods where we worked cutting trees and draining the swamp. Ten months of the year it was snowing. Ten months! Then one or two months without snow, and daylight for twenty-four hours. Every day I prayed. I was praying for my mother. I was praying for my brother—I didn't know that he had already been killed. I was praying for his children.

At five o'clock every morning we woke up and were given a small bowl of rice or gruel. Then the soldiers took us out to work. Every day we walked ten kilometers there and ten back—all year, even in winter. All the time I was working, I was praying. All the way there and all the way back, I was praying.

When they sent me to the prison, in one way I was happy. When I looked around me I saw so many innocent people. They had done nothing wrong. Maybe one of them told a joke or criticized Stalin. It was good for me to be there because I felt like I belonged. Strictly speaking, I was not innocent. I had supported my brother. I only helped him once, but I believed in him.

I didn't have any hate in me for my captors or the government. I had a deep pain inside, as though my heart was always hurting. But not hate. I'm surprised when I see other people who have been in Siberia. When they speak they are full of hate. But I'm happy I was there. My only sorrow is that my brother is not alive. He is not here to witness that his words came true.

When I think about my youth, I imagine what my life would have been like if they had not sent me to prison. I lost those years. I think about what might have happened and I have so much pain. Only pain, but not hate.

In prison I always had big, big hope. I knew that everything would be okay in the end. I was always telling my friends, "The time will come. Our lives will change. It will not always be this way." My nickname was "The Idealist." All those years in Siberia, I was trying to take something from life, to learn something. I practiced my Russian. When I saw someone doing something interesting, I would try to learn from them. I learned about medicine. I read big books and practiced mathematics. I was very active playing chess. When they had a competition between the women in the prison, I won first place.

Though prison was hard, the people there were the best people of our country. They were the thinkers, the scholars, the artists and poets—some of the most moral men and women. They were the ones who dared to speak out against injustice. It was a profound and even joyous experience to be among them.

I stayed in the prison four years and eight months. It was only because of my Heavenly Father that I survived. Only my faith and my prayers saved me.

⁓

At the time of Stalin's death in 1953, the government was giving amnesty to some of the prisoners. They were asking us questions and just letting some of us go. But not me—they were not going to let me go yet.

In 1956, I was called in a second time before a panel of nine people. They started asking me questions, so I told them my story. They asked me, "What do you think? Was your brother right? Did he do the right thing or not?" I said, "Yes, I think that he did right."

One of the nine did not want to let me go. They said they'd release me only if someone from the outside would write a letter stating that they would be responsible for me. I told them I would not agree to that. I wasn't guilty and I knew it. I said, "Who's going to write a letter like that? Maybe that person is more guilty than me."

I told them, "I'm not guilty of anything. I want to be a normal citizen, and if you think I'm guilty just shoot me. I don't want to live without any rights. And I don't want to speak with you any more because nobody will understand me."

Another one of these men had once been a prisoner. He said, "No, don't think that way. I was in prison, too, and I understand you." This old man said he knew my case. He knew that I didn't have any relatives to write a letter for me. My brother had been killed. I didn't know where my mother was. So he said, "I'll write the letter for you."

In the beginning, there had been four thousand women in the prison, and now there were only forty remaining. One day I kneeled down on the floor and started crying. I couldn't take any more. It was very hard on me. I prayed, *Please open one window for me and help me to get out of this prison.*

And it was the next day that the panel called me back again—my birthday, July 6th. They asked me, "If we let you go, what you will do?" I said, "I wish to go to Armenia, to Yerevan. I'm going to continue my education." So they said, "We have decided to let you go, but we are not going to give you amnesty." They let me go. No amnesty, just an early release.

I think that I needed to go through this experience. I know that everything that happened, happened by Providence; God's hand was in this. The years that I spent in prison . . . it was like a big school. All the people who went through this school got cleaner inside. It was a purifying experience.

⁓

I believe it is Heavenly Father's will that we experience everything that happens. After prison, I found my mother back in Armenia. I asked her about these things. "You and Father were such kind and honest people. Why does this happen to us? Why is Heavenly Father punishing us so, giving us so much suffering?" My mother said, "Jesus Christ was Heavenly Father's son. You know his father loved him so much, and yet he went through all his sufferings, too. Don't think that we are suffering so very much, and don't think it means that Heavenly Father doesn't love us."

After that I always remembered that Heavenly Father gave all the trials to his son, all the pain, and Christ sacrificed himself for the people. This always helps me when I remember my brother. He gave his life for others.

My advice to others is that when they have hard times—and there will always be hard times—be still. The first thing to do is pray. Always pray. And have faith and hope. When my son came to America it was hard for him. I would always write in my letters, "Please be patient, and always remember how your mother spent five years in prison and the conditions she endured. Always lay your burdens on Heavenly Father. Always trust Heavenly Father. Always pray and always have faith."

One day when I was in the prison, they took a group of us to the kitchen to peel potatoes. A couple of the women wanted to steal some potatoes and take them back to our barracks to eat. I said, "You can't do that; you are going to steal our friends' food. I'll not take part in stealing." They laughed at me, called me an idiot, and they took the potatoes. Later, when they were eating, they offered me some. I said, "No, I'm not going to eat. I won't take from the others."

There are many episodes from my life where I could choose to go the easier way, but Heavenly Father always helped me choose the right way. And when you are doing something good, something for others, you never need to announce it—just do it quietly. When we help someone else, we help ourselves.

Interview by Kent Miles
April 19, 1997
Salt Lake City, Utah

ANNE PERRY *is an enormously popular author of Victorian mystery novels. She has more than twenty-five million books in print, consisting of fifty-five titles. In addition to telling a good crime story, her novels provide insight into the roles of women and the class system during the Victorian era. Her books are currently being published in English, Italian, German, Japanese, Portuguese, Spanish, French, Greek and Russian. 2009 marks the thirtieth anniversary of her first published book.*

Anne Perry

Mystery Novelist
Ross-Shire, Scotland

I was born in London and grew up in England during the Second World War. I still vividly remember standing in the back garden and seeing tracer bullets from fighter planes above and, of course, hearing the sound of the air raid sirens. My father was a nuclear physicist, astronomer and mathematician. He worked with Sir Ernest Rutherford at the Cavendish Laboratory in Cambridge.[1] The Rutherford team helped lay the groundwork for splitting the atom and the eventual development of the atomic bomb. Because my father was a scientist, he would have no truck with religion, but he enjoyed music and art. In retirement, he loved to find

1. Called the father of nuclear physics, Rutherford discovered the structure of atoms and was awarded the Nobel Prize in 1908.

antiques, restore them, and then take them to the auction at Christie's in London. He would always give the proceeds to charity.

I came to the United States in 1967 on a work visa that only permitted me to look after children. I accepted a job in Southern California, where I met the neighborly Ray Barnes family. They introduced me to the LDS Church and put me in touch with some missionaries. The Barnes family made it possible for me to understand the fundamentals of the gospel, although if I had not already been searching I would not have been receptive to the truth.

I must admit, I gave the missionaries fits with my endless questions. Ray Barnes finally told me that I could not argue it out in my mind. He told me I should get down on my knees and ask the Lord for guidance.

I took his advice. When I retired to my bedroom that night, I knelt down and asked the Lord if the Mormon Church was the true church. Nothing happened. So I drifted off to sleep. When I awoke the next morning, a radiance filled my room to such a degree that I realized I had been given a sign. The illumination was far greater than the natural morning light. It was unlike anything I had ever seen before. My questions were no longer important and the way was made clear for me to see the truth and feel the Spirit. I told the Barnes family I was ready to be baptized.

In 1986, while living in England, I had the good fortune to meet Elder Russell Nelson of the Quorum of the Twelve Apostles.[2] Elder Nelson

---

2. One of the principal governing bodies of the LDS Church.

and his wife had come to England for the sesquicentennial of the LDS Church in England, and I had been asked to show them around Suffolk. I was nervous about carrying out this responsibility, in part because of my car. It was a banger of a motor, held together by hope and elastic. Meeting Elder Nelson, however, ended up being very important to me.

Several months later, I was in Salt Lake City on a book tour and I met with Elder Nelson at his office. I told him I had some questions concerning my purpose in life. Should I be writing for the Church or for the world? Elder Nelson gave me a blessing, and I had the clear understanding that I was to write for the world. I have tried to live up to that understanding ever since then, and I believe a good deal of my success followed that blessing from him.

My first novel, *The Cater Street Hangman,* was published in 1979. I was in my late thirties and had already been a struggling writer for twenty years. I believe my success comes from sheer determination and tenacity. You have to be willing to pick yourself up and start over again. You can't give in to disappointment. My material was rejected time and time again. I ended up revising my early manuscripts more than a dozen times. My first ten years of trying to live as a writer were years spent living on bread and water. The next ten, I lived on bread, water and cheese. Now I can finally afford some nice things. But when you achieve success you should never, ever forget the process that made all of it possible for you. That will keep you humble.

Unlike the grace of God, which is given to us, success is something you have to work for. You must be willing to make the necessary sacrifices. You cannot have joy in something unless you have paid the price. My goal was to be a good writer. I passed up parties and invitations to achieve that goal. I sincerely believe the Lord will make it possible for you to do what you are appointed to do in this life, but you must be willing to discipline yourself. You must not taint your success by compromising; always be willing to learn and stay with it until you have it right. Then you can have the satisfaction of knowing you have done your best.

I write every day of the week except Sunday. I begin at about nine in the morning and work until five, with a short break for lunch. In the evening, I begin writing at seven and finish around midnight. I write with a pen and have my work transcribed. I then read and discuss everything with Meg MacDonald, my friend and neighbor. Meg helps with story ideas and continuity. In one novel, I had a child sit on a chair to put on her shoes. Meg, a mother of four, informed me that young children sit on the floor to tie up their shoes. It's a small detail, but Meg's input is indispensable. It lends a certain authenticity to my work. My brother is my research assistant, and his experience as a doctor and army surgeon is invaluable.

Wealth is a great responsibility. You have to be very careful how you use it. For me, the most poignant story in the Bible is Lazarus and the rich man. It holds a personal message for me. When you have some success, the Lord will someday ask you what you have done with it. You must be able to answer that you did something worthwhile. I feel happy to share my wealth with those who are less fortunate and to encourage young people to discipline themselves.

Mormonism has given me far more than I have ever given it, in blessing my life and bringing me the love, mercy, and understanding of Christ. I served for a time as a Relief Society president and that was an important experience. I became involved in other women's lives. I had to understand and love them. That was not always easy, but it was what the Lord wanted me to do. I really came to a new understanding of human nature. It made me a better person, and it helped me immeasurably as a writer.

In a religion that values motherhood, I do not feel out of place as a single woman. Giving birth to a child is only part of the role of motherhood. I believe it is a woman's proper role to nurture everyone, to reach out and to help. We must give sustenance where it is needed. God does not ask of you something you are not capable of doing. If you do not have children, then there is probably something else for you to do in this world. There is some other mission, and you must prayerfully seek the Lord's way.

It is important to decide what kind of a person you want to be and select the three or four virtues you would most like to have. I feel the three greatest virtues are courage, compassion and integrity. They encompass all of the great virtues. If you strive to have them you will find peace of mind. Courage is the centerpiece of these three, and not enough is said about it. Examine all the great leaders of the Old and New Testaments and other scriptures—they all had great courage in their convictions to do what they knew the Lord desired of them.

Interview by James Kimball and Kent Miles
December 29, 1996
Portmahomach, Scotland

KIYO TANAKA *grew up speaking and signing in Japanese. Both of her parents were deaf and they taught her and her siblings sign language at an early age. Today, she anchors a television news broadcast in Japan for the deaf, conducted in sign language. She also works as an interpreter for the deaf, teaches sign language classes, and gives lectures about deaf culture. She currently lives in Yokohama and has six children.*

Kiyo Tanaka

News Anchor for the Deaf, Sign Language Instructor
Yokohama, Japan

I was born on May 31, 1948, in Yokohama. My father was born in Nagoya in the thirty-seventh year of the Meiji era[1] (1904). My mother was born in the fortieth year of the Meiji era (1907) in Tokyo. Both of them had hearing disabilities. They were profoundly deaf as a result of sickness. My father had diphtheria and my mother had a middle ear infection. I am the youngest of five children. I have three older sisters and one older brother. Because both of my parents were deaf and could not hear or speak, they taught us all sign language.

1. The period marking the reign of Emperor Meiji, 1868 to 1912.

My father sewed sashes for kimonos. By the time I was born he already had some young women living in the house as apprentices. There were seven or eight of these seamstresses, all of whom were also deaf. My mother could sew kimonos, too, but there were already so many seamstresses, and she was really busy with her children.

On the side, my father did a lot of volunteer work for other deaf people. He was the leader of a deaf association and was very involved in the deaf movement, which worked to improve the lives of deaf people. Because he was in a leadership position, deaf people would always drop by the house. My mother was busy waiting on everyone from morning to night.

My parents passed away about fifteen years ago, and what I remember most about growing up is that my father worked hard for other people. He was a really kind person—to anyone. My mother was a strong and powerful lady, someone you could rely on, an ideal woman.

Because our family communicated through sign language, we were different from my friends' families. My parents could never come to parent-teacher meetings. I might have been a little lonely at those times, but when I would go home my father and mother were so much fun. My mother had a great sense of humor. She was also very good at expressing her love to us. So outside of the home we were different from everyone else, but inside we had a wonderful, loving environment.

I was always sad when people who didn't understand us would be rude toward my father. That happened often. When he would ask people for help with something and they found out he was deaf, they would joke and say humiliating things to him. At school I would get teased because of my parents. One time some boys threw rocks and chased after me, yelling insults about my parents. I was really sad and frustrated and I cried my way home.

I couldn't yell, "I'm home," to my parents. You had to walk right up to them, face to face, and sign to them. On this particular day, my mom noticed that I had been crying and asked me sharply, "Were you made fun of at school today?" I couldn't tell her that I was teased because of her, so I denied it. My mother, for the first and last time, kneeled down and put her head to the bamboo floor and apologized to me. "I'm sorry, I'm sorry. You're getting teased because I'm deaf." I was only in the third grade, but I knew it wasn't my mother's fault. Because of those experiences I came to respect and love my mother even more. From that time on it wouldn't bother me when people said mean things to me.

When we had difficulties or disappointments, my father had a habit of saying to us children, "Forget about all that." So when I run into a wall or some kind of challenge, I forget about it and keep moving forward. There's no point in worrying when there's nothing you can do about it. My mother would always say, "Put up with it. If you endure it now, it will change for the better somewhere down the road." Since they were deaf, if something bad happened, often all they could do was forget about it and keep going. They were both so strong-willed. That was their way of getting through life and that's what they taught us. It was good advice, but I didn't understand it until I became an adult.

My mother went to a Christian church for deaf people. When I was little she attended services often. But at some point when I was in elementary school she stopped going. She was just too busy with things at home. When the Mormon missionaries came and visited our house, they gave the discussions to my mother and we translated for them.

In the end my mother didn't join, but my sisters and I did. She encouraged us. She had a Bible and would always take it with her to church. When I asked her why she went to church, she told me about the scripture in the Bible where Jesus says to the weary, "Come to me, and I will give you rest." My mother said you don't need to become Christian, just go to church.

That was about forty years ago. My parents really supported us in the Church, but they liked to eat and drink what they wanted, so the Word of Wisdom was difficult for them. They would go to Christmas parties and big conferences where traditionally there was alcohol.

What really attracted me to the Church were the many wonderful sisters. I had this vague feeling that I wanted to become a better person. I really looked up to the sisters at church and wanted to become just like them. They all smiled and looked so kind. They were more than missionaries to me. We were friends.

Now, forty years later, the Church is a part of my life. But I don't think I'm a very diligent Mormon. I started going to church when I was in junior high school. I had a lot of friends at church, so it was really fun. When I got into high school my father would take me along with him to gatherings with other deaf people. He'd often invite me on Sundays. And why do you think he brought me to these gatherings? He liked to brag about how I could interpret. That was fun for him. He would invite me even though he knew I had to go to church. Since he enjoyed it so much, I would go with him. Other deaf people would really enjoy it when I interpreted for him.

I knew that going to church and studying about Heavenly Father was important, but there was a time when I started to think that going with my father was more important. My older sisters saw me doing this and got worried. They thought I might become inactive.

When I was in high school I had a half-hearted attitude towards the Church. There was a sign language club that asked me to teach. They met at nights, so I went even while I had a full-time job. They had a lot of activities on Sunday, too. I was always confused as to whether I should go to the sign language group or to church. At that time, my sisters and I were about the only interpreters around. So I was always stuck between a rock and a hard place. In the end, I went to the sign language group more than church, and naturally, my sisters were all very worried.

In 1970, my sisters made a trip to Salt Lake City. They tried to take me along, but my mother was against it. She said that if something happened to the plane, it would be too horrible to lose all three of us at the same time. So I stayed home. In that same year—the year of the world's fair in Osaka—I went by myself to the Hawaii Temple. My sisters ordered me to go. They told me that I needed to become more humble and going to the temple would help. So I went to the temple when I was twenty-two.

During that trip I realized that I wanted to get married in the temple. I wrote a letter to my future husband, who was just a friend at that time, and told him that I would never marry anyone who didn't hold priesthood in the Church. So he joined, and we were married in the forty-sixth year of the Showa era[2] (1971).

The things my mother taught had a strong impact on me when I was raising my own children. When I thought about what kind of household I wanted to build, I thought of how I was raised; how I would come home to be greeted by a smiling mother in a house where I felt at ease.

They say your home is a little piece of heaven, but it can't always be like that. Ever since the kids were little, my husband and I have made a point to have family prayer and sing a Primary song together before the children went to bed. Then we would sit and reflect on the day—what kind of

---

2. The period marking the reign of Emperor Showa, known in the West as Hirohito, 1926 to 1989.

mother I had been, what kind of father he had been. I had a strong desire to raise my children in the Church. I didn't have the confidence that we, just as parents, could raise our children to be good. But with the help of the gospel we could teach them.

~

The Japanese are an earnest people. When we are told to do things like go to church or pray and read scripture, we follow it to the letter. But there are times when some things are accepted too well by society. When that happens, the serious people get really worried and frustrated. For example, they say to keep the Sabbath a holy day, so I would always wonder, *What's more important, going to church and praying or going to a volunteer group and helping others?*

I decided that if I was really needed by the group, then I wouldn't go to church that day. I still have a disagreement about that with my children. They can't believe that I go to work instead of church. I don't do the interpreter job anymore, but I still give a lot of lectures. When I go to lecture somewhere on Sunday my children say it's the wrong choice. Within the Church I've never been criticized, but I might have been seen as someone who isn't so active.

That said, being Christian is a part of my life and that will never change. I want to help families that are in need. I want to pass on the treasure of sign language that my parents gave to me. I really value my connections with the world outside the Church.

After I graduated from high school I didn't go to college. I was asked to start teaching sign language to a volunteer group. I also worked for the city of Yokohama as an on-call interpreter. For instance, if a deaf person needed to go to the hospital, I would be called in. People were always so grateful, because with the sign language my parents taught me, you can express emotions and feelings, as well as basic information. So that was my original job.

Now I teach a variety of classes, both professional and volunteer, and I'm invited to give speeches about sixty times a year. I also anchor a television news broadcast for the deaf. If you can picture it: just me standing there, on TV, signing the news.

～

My husband has a habit of saying, "I joined the Church just so I could marry my wife." I met him at a sign language group and at that time he was an eager believer in the Tenri[3] religion. I thought it would be really difficult to introduce the gospel to him because he was so involved in Tenri. I brought him to a church conference and he heard a great talk by Elder Yoshihiko Kikuchi, a Mormon general authority. His heart was turned toward the Mormon religion, and after some work and study he was baptized.

I tell my daughters that it can happen to them, too. They don't have

---

3. A monotheistic religion founded in the 1830s, also known as Tenrikyo.

a chance to meet many men outside of the Church. Right now I'm worried about my oldest daughter, who is twenty-seven and isn't yet married. She wants to have a lot of children, like me, so I tell her that she needs to get married fast. I also tell her that she needs to become more financially independent. Once she gets married and has her own family, then it's okay to stay home with the children and take care of the house. But she needs to become financially stable first. I always encourage my daughters to have skills so that if something happens they can take care of themselves.

I always had my husband discipline the boys. I would tell him that I couldn't raise boys. I could do things like feed and clothe them, but obviously the father has the greater impact on them. I would tell my boys only one thing: always be nice and gentle to women. It is important that they grow up respecting women.

When I was little, I always knew that my parents loved me. They didn't come out and tell me in words that they loved me, but I knew. So I have loved my children the same way—sometimes I even tell them verbally! I've always tried to let them know I love them. That's the most important thing—that they know they are loved. When my family lives a life in accordance with the gospel, we can live in total peace with each other.

⌢

Just recently at a ward in Tokyo, there was a deaf investigator who had been attending church for a while. They had people who could sign, so we usually weren't needed. But this man was going to get baptized and the missionaries were concerned that he really understood everything he was being taught. We were invited to go and talk with him. My husband and I went, and the investigator just started pouring out all the feelings he had since coming to church. I could understand him fully, so he wanted me to let everyone know the depth of his feelings. He wanted to talk to everyone *more* and express the love he felt for them.

As much as deaf people would like to talk to other people, to tell them how they feel, it is difficult to convey complex emotions. There aren't many interpreters who can really understand complex things in sign language. Through me, these people express what they feel, and I have the opportunity to interpret for them. At those times I feel fulfilled.

Whenever you use sign language you really stand out. People are quick to think that interpreters are special because they're always helping others. So you have to be humble, as it's taught in the gospel. My mother was the first to warn me about that. Even deaf people don't always understand some of the signs/words that I use. Sometimes it is difficult to be sympathetic to others—to not insult them. Mother told me never to make deaf people feel stupid. She encouraged me to take a step back and be humble. If I ever took a condescending attitude toward them, she would get really mad at me.

Because I've had the opportunity to meet all these people with disabilities, I know there are many extraordinary people among them. They shine. They lead wonderful lives, even with their disabilities. I have been extremely blessed to be around these people my whole life. To this day, I receive so much from them.

Interview by Kent Miles
November 9, 2000
Tokyo, Japan
Translated by Daniel Hick

CECILE PELOUS began as a young designer in the famous fashion houses of Paris—Dior, Cardin and Ricci. Every year she leaves the world of high fashion for the slums of India and Nepal, where she works to help impoverished children. In 1990 she founded an orphanage in Nepal, financed entirely on her own. The goal of her work is not merely relief aid, but to help people develop a self-reliant, sustainable way of life. In 2008 she was decorated by French President Nicolas Sarkozy as a Chevalier of The National Order of Merit of France.

Cecile Pelous

Fashion Designer, Humanitarian
Paris, France

When the Mormon missionaries came to my apartment door and knocked, I didn't let them in. Not until one of them mentioned they were from Salt Lake City.

You see, three years earlier I had been to Salt Lake City on a French student tour. I was so impressed with the city and its people (especially the Mormon Tabernacle Choir) that I came home and looked up everything I could about it. The books said they were Mormons and that they practiced polygamy, but I simply refused to believe it. The place had a spirit that was very holy. No city in all of the United

States impressed me so much. So when this missionary said he was from Salt Lake, I asked, "Are you from the church with the choir?"

I joined the LDS Church in 1975, after nine months of investigation. All eight of my brothers were opposed to it; they were Catholic. For a long time afterward, they said, "The Mormons stole my sister!" But in time they came to understand how much it means to me.

In college I wanted to be a teacher, but I had to sign a ten-year con- tract. I said I couldn't do that, so I began to study art, fashion and design. I then went to work in the fashion houses in Paris—Christian Dior, Cardin and Ricci. I started first at Christian Dior, then worked at the others, and eventu- ally came back to Christian Dior.

I was married, but we were unable to have children. We went through all of the difficult and painful processes to have them, but it did not work out. Eventually my husband and I separated. I found with the passage of years that I wanted something more out of my life. To me, taking fashion designs and implementing them into very expensive dresses for wealthy women lacked meaning. I felt deeply that there was more I could do.

I chose to take my vacation time and go to India and seek out Mother Theresa in Calcutta. When I first met her she asked me what I could do. I told her I was not a physician or a nurse, but I had been taught all my life to be of service to others. Mother Theresa said she understood. She told me to go to all of the Sisters of Mercy hospitals in Calcutta, as well as the orphanages and care centers. It was there, she said, that I would "find myself." At first, I did not know what she meant by this, but in time I came to understand.

I began visiting orphanages and I found my way to Banipur, a village in the Bengal region of India. When I saw the little children in the orphanages, I knew what I must do. Their sweet little faces and the hope in their eyes captured my heart.

A local welfare agency had built a chicken coop that provided one egg per week to each of the eight hundred children in the city's orphanages. One egg a week doesn't sound like much, but it was a precious addition of protein to a diet otherwise consisting exclusively of rice and lentils. Unfortunately, a disease had wiped out the chickens in August of that year.

When I got back to France, I said to myself, *If I return to India, it will be to rebuild the chicken coop in Banipur.* I went back to work at Nina Ricci and started saving money. It did not take me long to realize that my money would not be enough. I prayed. I told my friends and the president of the LDS stake in Paris of my plans. Three days later, I received a check from the stake, the result of a project named "Drop of Water," which the stake had organized several months prior to help relieve hunger in the world. The stake leaders had decided to donate the money they had raised to build the chicken coop in Banipur.

Donations in hand, I returned to Banipur in September 1987. I bought one hundred and twenty laying hens, a hundred and twenty chicks, thirty laying ducks, and enough grain to feed the birds for a whole year. I also bought six months worth of powdered milk for the children and materials to construct a chicken coop, which the villagers built.

I insisted on teaching self-reliance. Even the smallest child had certain duties in running the coop. In this way, they learned to feel responsible for one another's well-being. As a matter of fact, each orphanage has only two adult leaders and three cooks (who are disabled) to supervise one hundred children.

I noticed progress from one visit to the next. We transformed uncultivated land into a vegetable garden for the orphanage. At first, the children had no tools. They worked in the garden with wooden sticks. Today they have shovels and picks. Fish have been planted in the orphanage's little pond. Almost six hundred pounds of fish are harvested each year from that pond. Now each child can eat vegetables and eggs regularly, and fish now and again.

~

There is a Catholic priest named Gaston Grandjean who has chosen to live among the poor of India. He told me about the medical dispensary in the village of Belari. The dispensary was constructed to help the "untouchables," the lowest caste in India. After a road to the village was opened in 1986, people started coming for treatment from farther and farther away. The dispensary used to serve three thousand patients per month, but now it serves nine thousand. We have established a nursery, which cares for babies suffering from malnutrition. Mothers receive two hundred fifty grams of powdered milk each week for their babies and a free check-up by a nurse. It is amazing how much difference just a little supplement can make.

The villagers of Belari have also constructed a school for forty-five children. Men, women and children each brought bricks that they baked under the sun in the rice fields. I, too, made and donated bricks. Contributions help pay the costs of construction, the teaching personnel, and the cooks at the school. As a result, while helping their neighbors, some villagers are also earning a salary.

With money donated by some of the youth from the Paris Stake, a well has been sunk by the villagers and equipped with a pump. A second well with potable water is now in operation and infectious diseases have been reduced.

~

With each trip to India I was learning all the time. I knew I was doing good, but I felt there was something else, something more for me. In 1989, I found what I was looking for in the village of Nepalganj, Nepal, on the border with India. It is about five hundred kilometers east of New Delhi. There I found an orphanage for the neglected children of this poor country. It had almost nothing. It was just a hut. There was no running water, no electricity, no beds, and no medical care. It had no love. I couldn't turn away from it. That was the beginning of Asha Ashram, which means House of Hope.

I financed the purchase of the orphanage with my own resources. I sold my home and all my possessions and moved into a smaller house. Then we established a fundraising organization in France to help us underwrite our efforts in Nepal. Soon we also had non-profit organizations in Holland, Germany and the United States.

In the beginning there were nine children in the orphanage. They suffered from trauma and neglect, which takes its toll on the body and the spirit. When we began, the children had no hope beyond surviving through the day. Gradually, we built up a program and gathered in more children. Now we are finishing the construction of a two-story brick building. In addition to caring for these orphans, we have begun to educate them. Where there were once nine children, now there are many.

We would go throughout the country and find abandoned children and bring them to Asha Ashram. I found a young boy who had been abandoned, living in the jungle by himself. When we brought him to the orphanage, he slept on the floor even though he had a bed in his room. He once taught me how he made his bed in the jungle with leaves and small branches. He was like a small, tender, but wild animal. We taught him how to eat with utensils and read and write. Today I am happy to tell you he is at the top of his class at our orphanage school.

I go to Nepal twice a year for a two-month period. Nina Ricci graciously pays my full salary throughout these leaves of absence so that I will return and work for them the other eight months of the year. I know that when people have food to eat and clothes to wear they can then become interested in the gospel. I try to follow Church welfare principles. I obey Indian and Nepalese laws and I work through Indian organizations.

The first time I went to India I wanted to give a little of what I had to disadvantaged children. And I realize that in giving a little, I received so much. Serving them, I discover in myself talent and energy that I never would have sought for myself. I have been able to do much more than I thought possible, without previous training, but with the sincere desire to serve. I see that what I accomplish is part of the work of the Lord, and I am his instrument. He guides me and opens doors for me, sometimes in unforeseen ways.

I have contracted serious illnesses many times while in India and Nepal. After my first trip to Banipur, I was bedridden for nine months with paratyphoid.[1] But the Lord has given me the will and the strength to recover. There is still much work to be done. It is an unbelievable opportunity to be of service to young people. We're giving them a chance to better themselves, to learn to read and write and acquire a skill so they can lift themselves up from the only thing they have ever known: poverty.

Now we no longer have to search for orphans. They come to us. By word of mouth they have heard about our work and walk hundreds of miles to our orphanage. We never turn anyone away!

Each of us has work to do on this earth and responsibilities to our neighbors, far or near. We cannot, and must not, remain indifferent. We are blessed because we have knowledge and a marvelous personal relationship with our Heavenly Father. For me, that is my greatest capital. The surest

---

1. A fever contracted from unsanitary conditions.

way to make it bear fruit is to invest it in the service of others. This is a chain of unending love. Let's not wait for the Church to instruct us how to do good. If we lose ourselves in helping others, we will be blessed above and beyond what we can imagine.

Interview by James Kimball and Kent Miles
September 9, 1998
Salt Lake City, Utah

Eleven Years Later

Many things have happened since 1998. We built two brick buildings and a house for the Asha Ashram in Nepalganj. We furnished the rooms for the children. We dug a well for clean water. We taught them and cared for them. They began to grow up and their lives changed. We realized Asha Ashram would need to grow and change, too. We could only provide education up through the ninth grade. I wanted them to be able to continue their schooling. I felt that as my children grew up, my responsibility to them was not over. So we took them to Katmandu where there were more possibilities.

About five years ago, through our fundraising efforts in the United States, we met the people at Franklin Covey. They took an interest in our program. Many of Franklin Covey's employees have contributed to Asha Ashram and some have sponsored children, helping pay for their school expenses. Eleven of our students have gone on to work for Franklin Covey in

New Delhi. The director there told me, "It is an honor to receive your students from Asha Ashram. They are the best!" You see, I told my students when they left for New Delhi, "Please! You are the first. I hope you are not the last! I want you to be the very best at Franklin Covey. You have everything you need to succeed."

They arrived at Franklin Covey wearing their best clothes—clean shirts, ties, trousers and polished shoes. The other workers were wearing t-shirts, jeans and sandals. Now everyone at Franklin Covey wears shirts and ties. That is why they like to have the children of Asha Ashram. They have raised the bar for all of the employees.

I do not want to just care for my children while they are young. I want to continue to provide services. Let's educate them as far as they are willing to go. Let's give them work experience outside Nepal. Then let them come home and become leaders. Let them influence Nepal as they did Franklin Covey in India. These young people understand the problems in Nepal, so let's prepare them to become decision makers. They have the power to change and improve their country.

As any parent knows, since every child has different problems, we need to find different solutions for each one of them. Some children are very good students, so we work to get them into university. One of our children is finishing a mathematics degree in Australia. Another is studying to become a doctor at Katmandu University. Two of my children have joined the Church, and one girl is now on a mission, serving at Temple Square in Salt Lake. She is the first missionary to come from Nepal!

Some of our children have disabilities. For them, we have begun a new project to buy some land in Katmandu Valley. There, they can cultivate the land, grow fruits and vegetables, and become self-sufficient. In this way they all will have a positive influence upon their country.

Through the years, many people in other countries have expressed an interest in adopting some of the children of Asha Ashram. But that would take them away from Nepal and away from their people. I want these children to change Nepal in ways that will benefit all the people. The change may not come during this generation, but perhaps their children and their children's children will be the ones to see it. Why not? "The power is in [them] to do good" (Doctrine and Covenants 58:27–29).

To be honest, these children cannot be adopted because I have already legally adopted them. I have seventy-nine children. They are all now in my genealogy. Some years ago, we took in several children who had been orphaned when their village was flooded. A year later the village had been rebuilt and the local leaders came to Asha Ashram to reclaim the orphans. I hoped they would stay and get an education, but the government sided with the village elders. After that, I made sure I adopted the orphaned children so that they could not be taken away.

I retired from my fashion work a year ago and now I work full-time to support Asha Ashram and my children. They are no longer orphans. They have me and they have one another. They have a family now.

When I was young and married, we were not able to have children.

One of the reasons I first went to India was that I hoped to adopt an Indian child. But once I got there and saw the great need of so many children, I quickly realized it was not my way to help only one. If I really wanted to help the children I needed to give more time, more money, and perhaps start a home for children.

As time went by, I realized it was possible to give more. I discovered in myself a capacity I did not know was there. I discovered that when we are in extreme difficulty we search and find many possibilities. During my years in India and Nepal I was surprised that I was able to resolve the problems and the difficulties. I think that I grew up with my children there.

It is not finished, yet. Each day we learn.

I have learned that I am not important, but I am sure that the time and effort I have given has changed the lives of so many children. For me, it isn't necessary that I personally give life to a baby. I am a mother to a hundred and thirty-eight. But it took a long time to understand that, and for many years I was sad. I come from a family with eight brothers and they all have large families. Why should I not have children? But now I understand. If I had my own children, I would never have come to India and Nepal. And now I have more children than all my brothers combined.

Interview by Kent Miles
November 17, 2008
Salt Lake City, Utah

RAQUEL RIBEIRO DA SILVA CARVAJAO *grew up in an LDS branch in Brazil with fewer than twelve members. She married at a young age and dropped out of school. When her marriage went through difficult times, she reinvented herself through education. She opened a hair salon to support her children, finished high school, and went on to earn college degrees in social sciences, geography, history and education administration. Later in life, she was coaxed into entering politics and became a member of her city council.*

Raquel Ribeiro da Silva Carvajao

Teacher, School Administrator, City Council Member
Santo Antônio do Pinhal, Brazil

I was born on May 14, 1933. My parents have both passed away. My father was Antonio Ribeiro da Silva; he passed away in 1976. My mother was Leonilda de Lima Ribeiro. She was a special woman—one of the first members of the LDS Church in Sorocaba, Brazil. She was baptized in 1952. My father didn't want to go to church, but because of the constant example of my mother, after many years he was baptized. Eventually they were sealed in the temple.

After my father died, my mother did not remarry. In 1990 she came to live with me; of all her children, I had the most patience to take care of her. A few years later, she suffered a stroke. Then she had another stroke. She was bedridden for four years—she couldn't even drink on her own. I took care of her. She died on February 3, 2001. I buried her in Sorocaba.

When I was younger I didn't want anything to do with the Mormon Church. I didn't like the Mormons. I was Presbyterian. But my mother was Mormon and she was committed to her religion. I always had faith and I always had a strong love for God. I was always active in my church, I sang in the choir. But I wasn't interested in the Mormons.

One day I was at home—it was 1959—and I heard on the radio that over in India cows are holy. A cow is their god. I remember hearing that the milk of these cows was taken to temples and virgins bathed in the milk while little children went hungry. I got mad. I was extremely upset, and a voice said to me, *Why are you this upset? They were born like this. They don't know any other way of life, while you, who don't want to know of anything besides your own religion, are overreacting.*

I was disturbed because I knew from reading the Bible—I knew most of the passages in the Bible by heart—that there was one faith, one path, one baptism. I knew that some day I would be judged at the tribunal of God for the things I did and the things I left undone, and I began to cry. I knelt down and said a prayer with all of my faith. I asked God to have mercy on me, to help me, and tell me what to do. I didn't want to be condemned for something I didn't do simply because of my negligence or my ignorance.

I prayed for a while out of fear of being judged, and then the voice returned to me and said one thing: *Study . . . study.*

I resolved to ask my mother if she would send the missionaries to teach the discussions to me. I was already married at this time. My mother sent them over and they asked me, "Ma'am, will you pray to God to ask if the things that we're saying are true? If you have faith and ask without doubt, you will receive a response." So I did just that. That evening, I prayed and asked the Lord for guidance. I asked him to help me comprehend what the missionaries were explaining so that I could feel if those things were true or not.

We continued our discussions and my mind was opened. Many of the things I misunderstood were clarified. I studied. As an investigator, I was demanding. I asked so many questions; I wanted to know so many things. I studied for six months before I was baptized. It was a happy day. I was very emotional because I had been reborn. I had a new life with Jesus within the gospel.

⁓

The Church was very small then. At one point there were twelve people in our branch, and I got so excited because we had *twelve* members. That was in Sorocaba, and now there's a stake there. But it started with just a few of us—my mother, me, the elders. My father said, "Why do you go to this church when there's no one there? Go to the Presbyterian Church. It's right in front of our house, it's full of people, it has a choir and everything. You should go there." He didn't go to any church, but he told us to go there. My mother quoted to him, "Where two or three are gathered together in my name, there I am in the midst of them" (Matthew 18:20). And I felt the same as my mom.

I was baptized forty years ago, when I was twenty-seven, and I am now sixty-seven. I was married, but my husband didn't want to join the Church. We separated for a time because he liked to drink. He had a few issues like that. I stayed with him for ten years, and then I separated from him because it wasn't right.

He always wanted to return to me, but life with him was hard because we never had enough to eat. We were always in want and that was a hard life with kids. I had six children with him. Two of them died, and I stayed single while raising the other four. I also raised a student from one of my classes. We took him in and raised him and consider him one of our own. He went on a mission and everything.

My husband wanted to return and I told him, "Look, I am Mormon, and I'll only let you come back if you're Mormon. I want my family raised within the gospel." He said he'd listen to the missionary discussions and get baptized, which he did. But I found out later that he only did it so I would take him back. He really didn't have a testimony and he didn't want to go to church.

⌒

When I separated from my husband, I had to find a way to provide for my children without leaving them alone, so my mother helped me. She paid for me to go to beautician school. I did the courses and I bought a salon in the middle of Sorocaba where I could take care of my business and my children.

I was a successful beautician, but I thought I needed to continue to study. I had stopped school in the seventh grade when I got married. When I returned to school for the first time, I was scared just to talk to the secretary. It had been eighteen years and I didn't know anything. But as I began to study, I became more comfortable and confident. I attended high school with an emphasis in administration and I graduated at the top of the class. I even received a medal for doing so well.

After that I never stopped studying. I took the tests and began college. During my second course, I returned to my husband. He supported me during my studies. I went to São Paulo to enroll in my second course of study, where I majored in social studies. After this I did another college course in geography and then history. These courses of study are equal to college certifications in the U.S. After that I wanted to work in school administration, so I went and did a college course in education administration.

I was about forty-five years old by this time. I wanted to work in a school with both a first grade (equal to U.S. elementary school) and a second grade (equal to junior high school). I was a second-grade teacher. I liked the little kids, but I preferred the youth. Other teachers had more seniority than I, so I moved to Santo Antônio. I gave classes in history and geography on the high school level, and I also taught the elementary level. I taught them all.

The director of the school thought that I was very competent. She was going to leave and her assistant was taking her place, so they needed a new assistant director. She invited me in and asked, "Why don't you take the position of assistant director? It's a position of confidence; you would be the governor of the staff." I said, "Well, it's an opportunity for growth. I'd like to do it." That's how I got into administration.

～

I never thought about working in the political world, of being a politician. I have always worked in teaching and education administration. I never thought I would be a politician—never, never. But then a man, a doctor, came to my house and said, "Mrs. Raquel, you are a woman of good character—honest, hard working, always helping the community. I have followed your life and I came here to invite you to be a candidate for *vereador.*" That's a city council member.

I didn't think I had any business being in politics, but I went to the meeting anyway. All the candidates were there and they each had to announce their purpose or their intentions. I said I was there to support the mayor. Everyone asked, "I thought you were a candidate for *vereador?*" I said, "No, I'm not here for that. I'm only here to help the mayor," because I always like to help people.

One of my fellow candidates, a woman who was my friend, said, "You need to be a candidate because you are a special woman. Everyone likes you." I always want to help, and I thought that perhaps I would be able to be of service through this public office, so I resolved to run. I was afraid because politicians are always fighting within the party and with one another, and these people were all my friends. I was the only one from my party who ran for *vereador*, but I got along well with the others. We were a group of candidates who were excited and we represented change.

There were ten candidates for the council. I was the only one who didn't own a car. Most of the people in our district live in the rural areas. There are eight thousand people in the district, but only two thousand live in the town. I wanted to go to the rural centers—there is one well-populated neighborhood, José das Rosas, which had at least a thousand votes. I wanted so much to go out there, but I didn't have a car.

Then one day the mayor brought in all the candidates and announced that we were going out to José das Rosas together. "We are going to go on Sunday morning at eight o'clock. We will spend the entire day there and do a 'get to know you' campaign." I said, "I can't go on Sunday. I have a commitment. I have to go to church." And they said, "You can't think about church now. You have to keep your mind on the campaign. You'll always have church, but you only have three months for this campaign and then it's over." But I said I wouldn't go, I had to go to church. They all went to José das Rosas and I stayed behind.

But I won the election!

~

My husband died seven years ago. I am still fighting firmly and I am constantly helping in the Church. I conduct music and teach a class on family history. We don't have a branch nearby, so I leave the house at 6:45 in the morning to be there for the 9:30 meeting. The bus ride is more than two hours.

During all the years I studied, the thing that motivated me was growth. I wanted to be an administrator because I was capable. I wanted to be someone through my own efforts. I wanted to demonstrate not only to myself but also to my children that we *can*. I wanted to show the world that *I can*. You can't be afraid of change. You can, through your own efforts, arrive at where you want to go. You can grow. You can coordinate everything from work to your home. Everything. When you have the necessity to do this, Heavenly Father will grant you the capacity to coordinate everything.

There's an LDS scripture that says all the knowledge we accumulate in this life will rise with us in the resurrection (Doctrine and Covenants 130:18–19). I like that.

Interview by James Kimball and Kent Miles
March 15, 2001
Santo Antônio do Pinhal, Brazil
Translated by Matt Bowen

Christine Durham *is chief justice of the Utah Supreme Court, a position she has held since 2002. Prior to her appointment to the court in 1983, she was a trial lawyer. A graduate of Duke University School of Law, she has taught at Duke, Brigham Young University and the University of Utah. Chief Justice Durham has been recognized nationally for her work in judicial education and her efforts to improve the administration of justice.*

Christine Durham

Chief Justice, Utah Supreme Court
Salt Lake City, Utah

My father joined the LDS Church in Southern California when I was eight years old. The story is that he wore out two or three teams of missionaries. He finally joined when I was eight and I was baptized shortly thereafter. So I have recollections of my family's life before we became active in the Church.

Both of my parents were very hard-working people, and they both participated in the post-World War II boom. My father went to college and got his CPA by virtue of the GI Bill. His father hadn't even finished grammar school and worked for the railroad all of his life. I think his mother had a high school degree. Neither of my mother's parents had any significant education.

I recall that our association with the LDS Church resulted from a concern about education, about making the most of our opportunities, about doing whatever we did with a spirit of accomplishment and excellence. Growing up, I knew that despite my parents' relatively limited means, there was never any question that my two siblings and I were expected to go to college. My parents may have been a little startled that all of their children not only went to college, but went on to get graduate degrees. Well, that's how they raised us.

I grew up in a time of enormous growth for the Church in Southern California. I remember when the Los Angeles Temple was dedicated. I remember when stake conference meant that every Mormon in the entire southern part of the state came together in a big building downtown. I remember having general authorities[1] and members of the First Presidency come from Salt Lake for the conference. Even though I had been a convert, as a child I really had a sense of coming from the pioneer church. It was an inspiring time. I had a real sense of being different, of belonging to a peculiar people, and of having special obligations as a result of that.

My mother's family had once had a Church connection. In fact, she had been baptized as a child, but had never been active. Her family left Utah in the nineteenth century for the "real" promised land in Southern California, and she had been raised entirely estranged from the Church. It wasn't until after my father converted that she came back into fellowship.

---

1. Members of the First and Second Quorums of the Seventy, two of the highest leadership bodies of the LDS Church.

My father is a bright, hard-working man, but it was the Church that gave him a core to his life and enabled him to make sense out of it. The Church became a central part of our family's life.

My father worked for the IRS, and in the late 1950s we moved to Washington, D.C. In 1960 he was assigned to the Paris Embassy as a Treasury Department attaché. As I mentioned, both of my parents came from families of limited means and limited education, yet in 1960 we sailed across the Atlantic on a steamship with diplomatic passports and first-class tickets. We found ourselves thrust into the international diplomatic community in Paris. My brother and sister and I went to French schools, and our whole family learned the language.

The French LDS community in the early '60s was very small and anybody with experience was needed. Because we learned to speak French, we were asked to do a lot of things. My father served in the mission and district presidencies. My mother did everything. She ran Primary and Relief Society for a while.

In the early '60s, I went back to the United States to attend Wellesley, a women's college in New England. That was a significant experience. I had never been to New England, but I knew about Wellesley. It was famous as one of the Seven Sisters,[2] and it had very high academic standards. I knew it

2. Seven liberal arts colleges in the northeastern U.S., all of which were originally women's colleges: Barnard, Bryn Mawr, Mount Holyoke, Radcliffe, Smith, Wellesley and Vassar.

was a great privilege to go there. But my father was disappointed that I didn't want to go to BYU. As a convert to the Church, he always regretted not having the chance to attend BYU or go on a mission. He wanted that opportunity for all of his children, but most of us didn't cooperate.

I went away to college thinking I would like to distance myself a bit from the Church. During my teenage years I probably had more of the Church than I wanted because my family was so active. When I got to Boston, I thought, *Well, I'll keep my distance and have a little bit of an independent identity.*

As it turned out, I didn't know anybody in Boston. I was three thousand miles from home and family, and after a couple of weeks I thought, *I'll go to church and see some familiar faces and hear some familiar voices.* I ended up becoming quite active in the Cambridge Ward, which at that time was the only LDS congregation in the Boston area. Now, I think there are five or six wards and branches just in Cambridge.

My very first week in Sunday School, I was introduced to another LDS woman at Wellesley. She was a senior and she introduced me to a young man who was a friend of her family. He was a freshman at Harvard by the name of George Durham.

George was one of the few young men I had ever encountered—certainly so within the context of the Church—who admired me for having a mind and ambition, as well as a spiritual and personal side. Fortunately, I was smart enough to realize how rare that characteristic was. When he got back from his mission, he basically said, "Well, we either need to cement this relationship or end it." I said, "All right. Okay!" And we got married.

That was really a wonderful era in the Cambridge Ward. In those days, everybody was all thrown together into one ward. We had everyone from young Primary children to senior citizens, with the college students just sprinkled in. I found it a supportive and challenging place. Truman Madsen[3] was the mission president, and in those days the mission president in Boston taught Institute classes. Every Wednesday morning, we got to spend an hour and a half with Truman Madsen. When he was released, Boyd K. Packer[4] replaced him as mission president and took over the Institute classes.

So we had a really rich time of it. But historically, it was a difficult time. Many of the Church's policies on contemporary issues were very conservative. As students, we had lots of concerns and I was passionate about racial tensions. The Church's position on blacks and priesthood ordination disturbed me, as it did many of my generation. I became increasingly dissatisfied with the government's activities in Vietnam, while the Church took a conservative, pro-government position. So it was a time of much tension, and I feel fortunate to have found my husband, George, whose grip on the

3. Truman Madsen (1926-), New England States Mission president from 1962 to 1965, was a distinguished professor of religion and philosophy at BYU and an authority on Joseph Smith.

4. Boyd K. Packer (1924-), New England States Mission president from 1965 to 1968, is currently president of the Quorum of the Twelve Apostles.

iron rod is absolutely unshakable. It's not that he is insensitive to social injustice, or to irony, or to inconsistencies, but he has an enormous reassurance of all things spiritual. It keeps him grounded, and he helped keep me grounded during those years.

In the '60s, lawyers were changing the world, at least in this country. They were organizing assaults on racial segregation and attempting to change laws and practices that disadvantaged so many Americans. I saw lawyers as powerful instruments of social change. I never had any relatives who practiced law, or any connection to lawyers, and I'm not sure I was ever aware of even *meeting* a lawyer. So I'm not entirely sure where I got the idea that I should have access to power. But I did.

Wellesley had a lot to do with that. It has been in the business of educating women since the middle of the nineteenth century, so I was exposed to enormously bright, active women as classmates, companions and mentors. In that era, that was about the only place you could go to find women who were tenured college professors and leaders in their fields. So I had a lot of role models. There wasn't much overt feminism at Wellesley, but there was an unspoken assumption that women could and should develop their intelligence and their scholarly ability. There was an enormous emphasis (always has been) on making contributions to the community and helping other people.

So I came out of Wellesley with a strong sense of myself as someone who had an obligation to contribute and the ability to contribute. By my last year at Wellesley I had focused on a legal education as one way to do that.

Meanwhile, George was finishing his undergraduate work and applying to medical school. We had some enormous logistical difficulties, as he was a couple of years behind me. My first choice for law school was Harvard, but I got turned down. It's interesting to look back. I was aware at the time that some of my husband's roommates at Harvard were also applying. I knew of at least one, an English major, who didn't score as high on the LSAT as I did. He also had a lower grade point average than I had, but he was accepted. When I was turned down, it was just understood at that time that Harvard only admitted a certain quota of women, and to get in, those women had to have higher credentials than men. It didn't even occur to me to challenge those practices; they were just so much a part of the way the world was.

So instead I went to Boston College. This was after the birth of our first child, so we were juggling academic schedules and our daughter's schedule. When George finished at Harvard he got into Duke Medical School, so I had to transfer all of my credits and finish law school at Duke, which actually worked out very well. So we went to graduate school together in North Carolina. It's really hard now to imagine that time. When I tell young lawyers about it, their eyes just kind of glaze over; things have changed so dramatically.

I graduated from Duke Law School in 1971. It is a good school in Durham, a small town in North Carolina. I did well in law school, but there were only a half-dozen jobs in the vicinity that would even look at me. None of the law firms would interview women. Legal Services Corporation, a federal agency that offered legal aid, did hire women, but those jobs were full. So I ended up doing a lot of rather strange things. I worked for a law professor at Duke. I got a job at Duke Medical School teaching medical ethics and law to residents and undergraduates. All of these were part-time jobs, by the way. I did consulting services for an agency that provided protective services for the elderly, which was a new movement in the early '70s. I did a little bit of everything those two years while George finished his medical degree.

Those were difficult years. By then we had two children, so we were juggling them, and my work was very important toward supporting our family. I spent a lot of time feeling overwhelmed. I have to attribute the fact that I stuck to it to the wonderful relationship we had in our marriage. George was totally and completely supportive. From the day we were married, he always took the position that my career was as important to our relationship and to our family as was his. Consequently, we would make compromises, but they were not based on some automatic preference for his needs. We hoped for and worked toward a reasoned allocation of our resources.

When I got the teaching job at Duke, I had to create the course I would be teaching. It was very demanding, and George decided to take the summer off to care for our two little girls full-time. We laugh about that still. I would come home from a full day of work, tired and preoccupied. All I would want to do was sit down and have a few minutes of peace and quiet to read the paper and unwind. He would have spent the entire day with one toddler and an infant, not having seen another adult all day long. He'd be dying for some conversation, and he claims he gained ten pounds that summer by snacking off of their trays. It was all of the things that affect the typical housewife. It was a complete role reversal and it gave us a foundation for conversation, for empathy and understanding. We had so much of that overlap during the early years of our marriage, and I think it's carried us through a lot of difficult times.

George never took for granted what I was doing. He understood that it was costly and difficult, but that I was making a real contribution to the family. He claims that he simply came to marriage with the expectation that his wife would be an accomplished person, that the need for and benefits of accomplishment were not the sole prerogative of the husband. He was amazing. I dated plenty of Mormon men when I was at Wellesley. For the most part, I seemed to make them uncomfortable. While I didn't know exactly what I wanted to do, I made it clear that I wanted to do something. In addition to family and children, I wanted to work. I never saw the two as mutually exclusive. That may have been unusual. Prior to my generation, women who felt they had professional contributions to make tended to give up on notions of family and children. I never felt that way. It did not seem fair that women should have to give up one for the other, and George agreed. It was just never a question.

With George's medical school complete, we moved to Salt Lake. I began practicing law part-time, which was quite unheard of and rather bizarre. I joined a firm with a supportive senior partner who was very much a mentor to me. He was respectful of my commitments to my family and he let me work a part-time schedule. But it was a litigation practice, and things were getting progressively more difficult. I constantly worked half days. I'd run home in the afternoons and take care of the children. As soon as George got home from the clinic, I'd go back at night, and often on weekends, to try to catch up.

George thought he was in a position at the clinic to be able to cut back to part-time if I was ready to go full-time. So that's what we did. He cut back, and he was probably one of the first doctors in Salt Lake to work part-time. Now there are dozens. Just in his clinic, I know of three, all of whom are women, interestingly enough.

George has spent a lot of time taking care of children. He's changed diapers. He's walked the floor with them at night. Over the course of his career, he has commented on how much better a pediatrician he becomes with every phase of his life. Now, of course, we've started grandparenthood. We have grandchildren, and he said it's really put him back in touch with the phase of young parenthood that we had left behind.

We've been very lucky. Not long after we made the full-time/part-time switch, I had the opportunity to go on the trial bench. That would not have been possible with my hourly restrictions. So in many respects, I owe George just about everything.

I have the best job in the world, and frankly, if they didn't pay me to do it I'd have to figure out a way to pay them to let me do it. I like it that much. When people ask, "How do you do it all?" my response is, "Well, once you get used to coordinating the schedules of five kids and soccer games and music lessons and homework and laundry and all the things you do to manage a complicated household, managing an office looks relatively simple." My experiences as a parent and a partner increase my ability to do my job. When people ask, "Isn't it hard to be a judge and a mother?" I always say, "Being a mother is the hardest thing I have ever done." Being a judge is challenging, but it is not as hard as being a parent.

That said, work has its challenges. There have been times when I felt lost, especially when I was a brand-new trial judge. In those days they handed you a file and a robe and said, "Go be a judge." No training. No bench book. No backup. No nothing. The learning curve was very sharp. Nevertheless, I've always had a basic confidence about my ability to do what is needed. I look around and see other people who are doing the job and I figure, *Well, if they can do it, I can, too.* Whereas with parenthood, there have been many times when I felt like I was on the edge of the abyss, when I had no idea whether I could succeed, whether we would come through a difficult problem or a hard time, and I really had to operate on faith.

Wellesley has the Wellesley Center for Women. They do a lot of research on working women. They did a massive study on stress for women, the results of which came out in the early '90s. Their research thesis was that the more roles a woman attempted to maintain in her life, the higher her stress levels would be. In other words, if a woman was taking on the roles of mother, wife, sister and employee, her stress levels would be higher.

That thesis was not corroborated by the research. Instead, the key to stress, or lack thereof, was the level of satisfaction with the roles. So if you were doing more roles but liking it more, you had less stress than if you were doing fewer roles and liking it less. If your work provided a higher level of support, personal growth, encouragement, and spiritual well being, that was more important than how much work was being done.

I was pleased to see those results because they were consistent with my own experience. When we first came to Utah, I spent almost an entire year staying home full-time. I loved it. I adore my children. I love being involved in their lives. But the truth is, by the end of that year I was getting stir crazy. I was starting to feel dissatisfied with myself, with the kind of person I became in that setting. I felt much better about myself when I went back to work, even part-time. I felt better about myself as a parent and a partner by virtue of being a lawyer.

The contributions we make as a parent and a partner rely very much on faith. You invest your whole soul in the lives of your children and their success, but in the end you have no control over the outcome. So if your sense of self-worth comes from your children and their success, you're in deep trouble. Whereas in the professional world, you have much more control—you do a good job and you have the satisfaction of the product you've created. That balance has always been very helpful.

I have come to realize a couple of things about myself. If I had invested my identity entirely in my family-related world, I would have put my self-esteem at risk. And given the kind of person I am, I probably would have ruined my children if I had invested all of my energy in their lives. They claim they're neurotic enough as it is. If I'd been around twelve hours a day supervising their lives, the expectations would have been too much.

Which is not to say they don't also gripe about being deprived because of my career. My son claims I never made him cookies. Well, it's not true. I made him cookies, and when I wasn't there his father made him cookies. And at a very young age, he figured out he could make better cookies than either of us. And ever since he's made his own cookies.

Each generation must find its own way. When I was a young mother, the messages from the Church seemed largely irrelevant to my life: "Stay home and have babies and take care of your husband and your babies and that's it." Well, I was having babies and I was taking care of them, but I was doing it with the help of my husband. I wasn't getting much support from outside the Church, either, since I was doing things that so few had ever done before. I was the first pregnant law student in the history of Duke Law School. Not the first woman, but the first pregnant one, and people were kind of bemused by it. I mentioned that I had a hard time getting a job in North Carolina. Even when we moved to Utah in 1973, only one law firm in town even had a woman attorney, and at least one firm declined to interview me because I was a woman. It wasn't a welcoming atmosphere.

On the other hand, there was the exhilaration of being a pioneer. There was a sense of, *I'm going to do this and show you all.* Whereas, now my daughters still experience the same message from the Church in some respects—stay home and have babies—but they exist in an economic era in which the likelihood of being able to stay at home and still afford everything is considerably reduced. My children live in a secular world that tells women that they can have everything, that they should be able to do it all without blinking. In my profession, for example, there is no issue now about women getting jobs in law firms. But negotiating adequate maternity leave, staying on a partnership track, getting respect for their family-related activities, is every bit as difficult, and in some respects more difficult, than it was for me.

The secular world doesn't provide a George Durham. Or work-based childcare, or any form of maternal support. We see enormously punitive attitudes toward welfare mothers. George often points this out. We give a great deal of lip service to being child-oriented in this country, but we have the most regressive policies, or lack of policies, directed to children's welfare of any industrialized nation in the world.

One of the experiences that shaped our lives enormously was the birth and life of our daughter Melinda, who was born with Down syndrome. Melinda is a remarkable human being, but when she was born a couple of things happened. George brought me his medical school text on child development so I could look up Down syndrome. It reduced me to absolute jelly. It basically described these children as totally non-functional, requiring institutionalization—they wouldn't talk and they wouldn't walk. It was outrageous. It was an old text, but it was the one he'd had in medical school.

One of his colleagues, a woman physician, came to the hospital and said to me, "I guess this means you'll probably have to abandon your career. This child is going to need so much from you, I don't know how you can build a career and give her what she needs." So that was my introduction to the wonderful world of special needs childcare.

Both projections turned out to be entirely off base. Melinda has been on the cusp of a revolution in intervention in the lives of developmentally disabled children. As her parents, we have been very aware of the struggle to create those services, to fund them, and to make them available in the community. We've known a lot of the pioneers in this state, the people who did the hard advocacy work to bring it about, and we know the kind of battles they've fought and are still fighting. It has changed our lives in a dramatic way.

Being Melinda's parents, we learned that we were not self-sufficient. By definition, we were needy. No matter how educated, affluent, influential and successful we were in the community, we could not buy or create the things she needed in the way of services, education and opportunity. We were reliant upon structures outside of our family. We were reliant on social services.

That was an educational experience, and it has had a profound impact on my attitude toward what communities are and what they are for. For example, things like the so-called welfare debate. The modern American family cannot meet its children's needs alone. Period. We require a whole network of services for education, for socialization, for medical care. The notion that, somehow, the children of those welfare mothers are their problem and not mine is absurd. It's absolutely absurd.

With Melinda: she reads, she rides the bus, she works, and she's going to pay taxes—all because she had access to educational services. In another era she would have been sent to the American Fork Training School and supported at state expense all of her life. Those kids of welfare mothers out there, if they don't learn to read and ride the bus and hold down jobs and pay taxes, they're going to be supported by taxpayer money for the rest of their lives. As a public servant, I feel an obligation to make the system better, to serve the public better. George is the same in his profession, and he spends a lot of time thinking about these issues.

There is a clear connection between this professional/social consciousness and our personal approach to meeting the needs of our family. We didn't always fit nicely into the stereotypes that came out of Church culture. You know, the talks you hear and the *Church News* editorials about how no success can compensate for failure in the home. We would sit down, look each other in the eye and ask, "Is there any level on which we compromise our commitment to, and our coverage of, the needs of our family?" We could come away from those talks knowing that we had applied the principles to our lives, regardless of the appearance of non-conformity on the surface.

~

People often grow up in the Church assuming they're limited because of who they are—because they're female, because they're male. I see it all the time. I've taught in the Young Women organization and Relief Society, and I remember being distressed at the lack of emphasis on self-sufficiency and independence in women's lives.

In the early Church, the men would often be called to go on missions, leaving their wives as the sole economic support of the family. Women dealt with those expectations, which grew out of the economy and the community in which they lived. The thing that I find strange in this day and age is the degree of disjunction between the sanctioned expectations and the economic reality in our community.

I look at my ward. I look at my neighbors and friends in our Salt Lake neighborhood. We match all the statistics for divorced, single, widowed, never married; disabilities, chronic illness, mental illness. I mean, we're human beings. Globally, the Church has to fit into the communities and the economies in which it exists.

It is important to clearly perceive the difference between religious/spiritual messages and cultural expectations. To an extent, the so-called

American nuclear family—a Dad who works and a Mom who stays home with the kids—is an artifact. It was a model that was viable for a short period in America after World War II, and it hasn't been viable before or since. Yet at some point it was incorporated into our cultural perceptions about how the Church operated. I suspect that is partly because it was a period of such enormous growth and success for the Church.

I hear stories from people who have been out in the world working with Latter-day Saints in Africa and Bosnia and Russia. There is a couple in our ward that just came back from Siberia. Listening to them, you get a sense of inevitability about the Church overtaking itself. These converts bring their lives into the Church. Yes, their lives will be changed by the Church, but the Church will also be changed by their lives.

I remember having an intense discussion with Brother Packer when he was teaching Institute years ago in Boston. Speaking metaphorically, he said the youth always have a tendency to get very close to the edge of the cliff. The function of Church leadership is to give them direction and instruction that will keep them as far from the edge as possible, knowing they're going to move out closer anyway. The hope is that if the instruction starts here and they only move out so far, they'll still be far from going over the edge.

That was thirty years ago. I don't know if he remembers the metaphor, but I certainly still see it. I took issue with it back then. Now, after thirty years of parenting and mentoring, I see his point and I understand why the Church does what it does. But I also think it's very important that when you give people enormous challenges in their lives—asking them to do phenomenal things, which the Church does ask—you must also give them support.

The world changes so much from generation to generation. When I think back on my own life I realize how much that is true. Years ago, when I was teaching at BYU, I was invited to a dinner with some other young attorneys. One of them asked me where I practiced. I explained that I was with a small firm in Salt Lake that did securities work, and he asked me what kind of work I actually did. I said, "Well, mostly I litigate." He literally dropped his fork in the salad, and said, "Oh, my goodness, you litigate? You go to court?" "Yeah."

He went on to say that he was the pre-law advisor at BYU. He was actively recruiting women to the law school and recruiting women into law generally. He felt there were all kinds of places for women to have a wonderful role in the profession, but it had just never occurred to him that the courtroom would be one of them! Now, I know that since then he has changed his perspective considerably. But at the time, my life challenged his assumptions. That was not an uncommon experience, and it shows how the world has changed in my lifetime.

I've spoken mostly about what happens to the young women, but the problem is equally serious for the young men. They are being raised with expectations about the women in their lives that are obstacles to the kinds of partnerships you hope Mormon families would develop. They are also raised with the expectation that they have to provide a certain level of financial stability, and that they have to carry that burden all by themselves. But the money should be of secondary value. My son Troy isn't married yet, and I'm interested to see what kind of a woman he looks for and what kind of a partnership he forms.

I remember when Troy was about eight—I got home late, George was cooking, and Troy followed me up the stairs and said, "How come Dad does most of the cooking?" I said, "Well, mostly because he gets home first, and he just does." Then Troy said, "Yes, but moms are supposed to do the cooking." It had just dawned on him, at age eight, that it was a little odd that his mom didn't do most of the cooking. It was just something he had picked up from friends at school. I sat down with him and we talked about why.

It works the other way, too. When Jennifer was five, she found out her uncle was a lawyer. He was working in the family furniture store, so he wasn't practicing, but she found out he was a lawyer and she looked at me and said, "But I thought only mommies could be lawyers." So it works both ways.

I remember when the LDS Church came out against the Equal Rights Amendment, the proposed constitutional amendment. I had been active in that cause back when we lived in North Carolina. I studied the amendment in law school and decided it was a good thing. I did some lobbying for it, both in North Carolina and here in Utah. In fact, I spoke in favor of ratification in front of the Utah Legislature, right about the same week the *Church News* editorial came out condemning it. Perfect timing!

People would ask me, "How can you support this when the Church has taken a position against it?" I never developed a totally satisfactory answer to that question, except that I was making an effort in every area of my life to meet all the fundamental obligations I felt were part of the gospel; namely, in my marriage, my family and my personal relationship with God. It seemed to me that if I were able to do that, then I could make an assessment about a very complicated political, historical, social question. I don't know, maybe my attitude was, *Well, if God doesn't like my position, he knows where I am. He can find me, and since he hasn't so far.* . . And of course, the whole issue went away because we lost so miserably.

I know my position created discomfort for other people, but not for me. I had a sense that I was in the right place at the right time, doing the right things. I'm sure there was also a certain arrogance of youth. I felt like I knew a lot more about the Equal Rights Amendment than some of the people who were criticizing it. I had read it more, studied it more, long before it became a public issue. But I did have a wonderful experience when we had Utah's International Women's Year convention in Salt Lake City in 1977. I got to debate the Equal Rights Amendment in front of eight thousand people, most of whom were not happy with my side of the debate.

⌒

I've been a justice on the Utah Supreme Court since February 1983— a long time. As of this week, there are apparently seventy-one women on state supreme courts. When I first came to the court, there were thirteen. I was number thirteen, unlucky number. So that's been a dramatic change in that period of time.[5]

After feminism reached the legal consciousness, there was the notion among many judges that if women want to be equal, fine. Everything will be split fifty/fifty. But I was the one with the motivation to go look at the earnings tables and point out the economic reality of women's lives. Often a fifty/fifty split wasn't fifty/fifty. I was motivated to do that because I am a woman, because I was interested in those issues, and because I had some experience of being disadvantaged in the commercial world because I am a woman. But it wasn't just me. I could never do anything around here without two other votes. Sometimes it's just a question of having the motivation to ask a question differently, and to look for information that might not appear on the face of the case.

I love the intellectual stimulation of being a judge. It's kind of like solving puzzles, and I do enjoy being a problem solver. In a wonderful article called "Violence and the Word," the opening sentence is, "Legal interpretation takes place in a field of pain and death."[6] The article goes on to point out that judges make these rulings; we write them in opinions and publish them in books. But once the rulings have been made, someone goes out and enforces them. Someone takes someone else to jail. Someone takes some-

---

5. Since the time of this interview, another woman, Jill N. Parrish, has been appointed to the Utah Supreme Court.

6. Robert Cover, "Violence and the Word," *Yale Law Journal*, 95: 1601–30 (1986).

one's children away. Someone evicts someone from their home. A marriage is split; custody of children is allocated. I try to remember that. "Violence and the word" is a real stark phrase, and you can't live with it on a consistent basis, but I try to keep it in mind when I'm doing my work. I remind myself that it's not just an intellectual exercise, that we represent enormous power. We don't have power ourselves, but we speak for the state when we make our rulings, and the state has enormous power to change the lives of citizens, and not always for the better.

The older I grow, the more acutely aware I am that life is a process. One of my favorite sayings is "life is not a dress rehearsal." This is all you get. For me, it is increasingly meaningful to reflect where I've been and to project where I'm going. I look forward to another twenty years of that process, if I'm lucky. I would love to be a wise old woman. That would be a wonderful calling.

Interview by James Kimball and Kent Miles
March 11, 1997
Salt Lake City, Utah

EMMA LOU THAYNE *is a published author, poet and mother of five. She taught English and coached tennis at the University of Utah for several years. She gives lectures around the country to universities, churches and community groups. Her intense curiosity about life and her gift of language—both verse and prose—has won her numerous awards, including the prestigious Madeline Award for Distinguished Service to the Arts and Humanities and the David O. McKay Humanities Award from BYU.*

Emma Lou Thayne

Poet and Author
Salt Lake City, Utah

The great joy of growing older is that we get to look back and think about the people who have blessed our lives. In our home, where my three brothers and I grew up, we had an interesting combination of the athletic and the aesthetic, and what a balance that was. It brought such richness to our childhood. Here I was with my three brothers and my father, who was an athlete deluxe. He loved athletics, and started the Young Men's basketball program[1] in the Church. He was just as joyous in the world as anybody I've ever known.

1. A program of the LDS Church's Young Men's Mutual Improvement Association (YMMIA).

And then there was Mother, who was the aesthete. She was a tiny lady—only four feet, ten. She loved the beauties of life and brought them to our home. She was an artist, a painter and a writer. She wrote poems and had them all over the house. In our lunches going to school, there'd be a little verse of some kind. And she loved the ballet and opera—had the opera on every day, and we were influenced by that. They were quite a pair.

I was the only girl, and I had the best of two worlds. I had all the love, affection and culture any girl could want, and I could also be a tomboy and do all the things my brothers did. I learned to throw balls and run and climb trees, and then I could play dolls with my best friend every day. What a way to grow up! There was the expectation that life was good, that people were good, and that there were things to learn and benefit from. I didn't grow up in a house of criticism. There was this attitude: *Why not? Let's try it, let's see.*

Never Past the Gate was the first novel I wrote, which was published in 1975. It's the story about growing up in our summer home in Mount Aire Canyon. We'd go up there the day school was out and not come down all summer. We lived up there with this whole nest of cousins. "Never past the gate" was our promise, never to pass that gate until we came down in the fall. The whole book is about the times when the gate had to be passed—when my brother, Homer, was bitten by a rattlesnake; when another brother, Rick, was terribly ill and had to have his hip fused because of osteomyelitis.[2]

---

2. Osteomyelitis is an infection of the bone or bone marrow, caused by bacteria.

We became little earth creatures, living up there where everything was in tune. If there were rattlesnakes, they were just a challenge. It wasn't something that was dire and awful. It was a challenge to go up onto Rattle-snake Mountain and see what would happen. Everything was an adventure.

I wrote a piece for the *Ensign* called "Mother Killed the Rattle-snakes."[3] It was about the fact that my big, athletic father was afraid of rattlesnakes. My mother would go out there, armed with that shovel. We'd call Mother and she'd take care of whatever needed to be taken care of. It was a metaphor for the way they lived. They both operated from strength, not from weakness, and they brought a kind of wholeness to each other. It was a mighty influence for happiness later in our own homes, and continues to be.

My parents had two sayings. Mother's was, "Pray at night, and plan in the morning." She was a woman of great faith, which wasn't really talked about much. I never heard either of my parents bear testimony in a formal setting. We did not read scriptures among each other, we didn't talk philo-sophical kinds of things. They just acted on it. It was all so real that, of course, we wanted to follow their example. And Father's saying was, "Things work out." And you know, when you live with those two sayings, you have a pretty secure foundation to do anything you want to do. To me, they epito-mized what a Mormon family can be.

---

3. *Ensign*, April 1975. The *Ensign* is the monthly magazine published by the LDS Church.

We need to allow for the enormous potential that each human being has. I love the statement, "Become the full measure of our creation." I think my full measure includes many things beyond a gospel doctrine class. While the Church has to work for people all over the world who have no background in Mormonism, it does not seem profitable to reduce everything to the least common denominator, and the least *informed* denominator. That seems to do such disservice to the whole community of saints. The gospel has a depth and persuasion that can offer a life like my parents gave me. Our family's approach wasn't, *Watch me live my life.* It was simply, *Live your life!* Live it and love it and enjoy it and enjoy people. Let them in, and relish what each one has to offer.

People ask, "Do you write as a Mormon?" That's like asking, do I write as a woman? Do I write as a mother? All of these things are as inseparable as smoke and flame. They ask, "How do you accommodate your Mormonism? How does it fit with all the other things that you've been learning?"

I say, "The pillars of my faith are still intact, but the roof has blown blessedly off the structure to reveal a whole sky full of stars."

⁓

Each baby I have given birth to, or been privileged to hold as mother, grandmother, and now great-grandmother, has furnished me with the joy of belonging. That is my substantive spirituality. I have felt the connections to God, even as I have known so intimately my human connections to family.

I am a Mormon housewife who, for all of my life, has *had* to write. My culture is unused to sustaining two identities in any one woman. Mothers have been encouraged, almost by edict, to stay in the home and not pursue work that would take us away from our children. Even those of us on general boards of the Church—sent on weekend assignments around the country or abroad—were expected to leave casseroles in the freezer and clean clothes in the drawers.

In pioneer days, the esteemed Mormon poet Eliza Snow was accepted in her community, even called a priestess. But she was an exception. She had no family obligations and no children, even as she knew favor as wife of Joseph Smith and, later, Brigham Young. She was free to follow her muse. But most Mormon women exist in a web, a labyrinth of expectations.

My culture idolizes the simplified woman, ardent and singular, bent to the collective and determined to serve it. The idea of the radiant mother, which I have been a part of for nearly forty years, is not something I would abandon. But a concomitant life beckoned, the life of those poets. It's one of the great human dilemmas: How could I live both lives and be fulfilled without sometimes neglecting one or the other? Mostly by being tired in the morning.

Luckily, I almost always had more energy than time.

I've had five children, five darling girls. Having been a part of their lives has been my most transcendent experience, by far. Being up in the night with the baby, exhausted, was beyond privilege—the intimacy of just us. When he was home, my husband Mel helped generously with changing a baby or celebrating a birthday. But in those years he was mostly a visitor for dinner; a gentle, smiling man at the piano playing "Polly" to dance to, or hymns to sing together around the Christmas tree. He often said that being a realtor had all the demands and none of the privileges of being a doctor—appointments on Sundays and holidays and often at night. In addition, he taught real estate classes two nights a week to augment his earnings and satisfy his thwarted training to be a professor of history. And he needed his sleep.

We were always busy, and we were a good team. Through hectic schedules, crises, the repetition of housework and homework, I have been tired but never bored with mothering. If anything, it has gone too fast. And I have needed much less sleep than Mel.

At the same time, I realize I could never have given up a life of my own. My blood runs with a thousand interests and joys. I have loved my life. But as with any housewife, the demands could sometimes be suffocating. I grew up knowing how to keep the house tidy, the laundry done, and nourishing meals on the table, but my variety of interests could often be a burden to a teenager wanting to sleep in on a Saturday, or a child waiting to be picked up from a violin lesson. I always believed that quality made up for quantity, and that I could love them with all my heart, even if not with all my time.

When she was ten, our poet-child ended a poem, "When she's typing / You answer your own question."

While I'm sorry in my bones for that, I think my children have come to laugh about it, especially as they have become mothers themselves with many of the same conflicts of interest. We have stayed close through great fun and agonizing tragedies, in sickness and in health. Never has there been enough time. And for them, having such a busy mother was never easy. But when they have needed me, they know I'm there.

In my prayers, I've had to abandon my instincts to be a fixer, to learn, as my mother finally did, to be there with love, but then "let go and let God." In a blink those little girls grew into young women and were gone to lives of their own. After each moved on, I was left wondering where they had gone—the years, the bounty of a full house. We've shared the thrills and heartaches of dating, and later, a divorce. One by one, they have brought men into my life to love like my own. We share a mixture of laughter and anxiety over the challenges of making a living, or dealing with the vagaries of their families. We learn from one another. We share the saving grace Mother and Father bequeathed me and my brothers, a kind of situational patience that can be a balm for wounds, doubts, disappointments and trials.

~

Things happen and things work out. They come to pass, not to stay.

At home or away, dealing with what happens is most crucial to being part of that home. To ask why, or why me, can be the least productive of concentrations. Why *not* me? Why not *any* of us? The unpredictable in life is often the best teacher, the imperative of flexibility, the thing learned. It takes real faith not to pray, *Please, with your omnipotence, change all this*; but to ask, *Please, with your strength help me to manage.*

As times have changed, my women friends started going to school and taking jobs in government, nursing, real estate and education. For seventeen years, I served on the board of directors for the *Deseret News*,[4] alongside general authorities and presidents of BYU. I was the lone woman at meetings, living two lives, at home and away.

One year, we hosted the board's summer party at our cabin. Just hours before the party was scheduled to begin, we were all in the boardroom in the Church Office Building. While my body was seated at the table, I was mentally scrambling to make preparations for the party. The men in the meeting talked casually about picking up their wives. I joked, "I need a wife!" The men all laughed. They were not used to the notion that a wife would be anywhere but at home with dinner on the table.

Life drew me in a thousand directions. Years ago, longtime friends in Sun Valley, Idaho, offered me their empty condo in the off seasons. At age sixty-two, leaving town alone became a tantalizing option. Identity in mar-

---

4. The *Deseret News* is the Salt Lake City daily newspaper owned by the LDS Church.

riage can't always be as one. Mel's support, emotionally as well as financially, had always lent me a freedom I thrived on. Though he had been my most enthusiastic fan, convincing him of the critical importance of my time away was not easy. Who in our generation ever took such vacations from responsibility?

I had to convince him that my life was literally at stake—my inner life. Writing was like breathing, like his working life was to him. But what would people think? "If you or one of my brothers had to be away for your job, would anyone question it? Would they feel sorry for the poor wife left at home?"

Gradually, we made peace with my going. Mel learned to find enjoyment, too, in a new kind of retirement. He spent more time with his children and grandchildren, performed marriages in the Salt Lake Temple, and wrote his personal history. Though he is sometimes lonely when I'm away, we have discovered that time apart enriches our time together.

Out of those biannual trips to Sun Valley came a quiet solitude. It was like sinking into a spiritual realm I thought was reserved for monks. Up there, my head can go to the end of a thought, ideas can surface and be paid proper attention. I have come to know something of nirvana, the state of absolute blessedness, great harmony and joy.

Out of time alone came poems. Poems I could never have written from my usual consciousness. Poems to expand my seeing, and to look, as

Yeats says, "into that little, infinite, faltering, eternal flame that one calls one's self."[5] Going back to my usual life is a challenge, just as staying away too long would be.

~

A few years ago, Laurel Thatcher Ulrich and I were invited to go to Ireland with six other writers. We had no notion what this kind of trip would do. Oh, I tell you, it was most remarkable. I mean, what did *we* know about Ireland? You hear about leprechauns and fairies and all that sort of thing.

We found them all!

It was such an adventure—only twelve days—but you know what can happen in twelve days. The last morning, I woke up early and looked out the window to see what the weather was like. There was this *giant* rainbow! By the time I woke everybody up to see, there was a double rainbow. We had a beach of our own, when the tide went out, and this rainbow arched up from that beach just as if it were holding us in its arms.

Later that day, a friend and I were in Galway. We crossed over a bridge and there was this gorgeous stone cathedral—the Galway Cathedral of Our Lady Assumed into Heaven and St. Nicholas. A scattering of people

---

5. William Butler Yeats, from the dedication in his 1897 collection of stories, *The Secret Rose.*

were celebrating the Eucharist[6] in a small chapel. We passed through the chapel and entered this glorious cathedral, where we observed the Stations of the Cross.[7]

We sat in the very last pew and looked down this enormous chapel. My eyes were drawn to the stained glass windows facing west. Here came this light that threw rainbows against the stone pillars—just like the rainbow we had seen that morning! Further down, on the crucifix above the altar, there came a white light that illuminated Christ's face and the two figures below him.

"I can't leave until the light is gone," I said. It was just too remarkable—a sense of . . . *everything!* Just at that moment, beautiful music came into the cathedral. It was "Danny Boy." "That's my song!" I said to my friend. "I learned it on the piano from my father when I was ten. It's the only song I still know. It was played at my father's and mother's funerals, and it will be played at mine."

So here was this music, women singing in Gaelic, singing all three verses. We couldn't tell where the music was coming from, but if I've ever heard heavenly music in my life, this was it. And I knew the words in English

---

6. A Christian sacrament commemorating the Last Supper, also known as Holy Communion.

7. A series of fourteen pictures or sculptures depicting the final hours ("the Passion") of the life of Jesus.

so well that I could follow. As that happened, I was filled with a light that was like my father was there next to me. I sat there in a state that I had only experienced once before, when I had a near-death experience after a car accident. I sat there in this sate, and I couldn't do anything except bow my head and weep. The tears just ran the entire time.

My friend said that she watched me, and I am glad she was there to be a witness. But we decided later she was much more than a witness, she was a participant. She watched me for seventeen minutes, and I couldn't move. I consulted later with my Catholic friend in Tulsa. She told me that I was hearing something Catholics call "the music of the spheres." "That's something that we talk about and know about, but few people ever experience it." And I told her how I was filled with light, and she said, "Well, we have a term for that too, and it's called 'resting in the Spirit.'"

When the music stopped, I couldn't move. As I opened my eyes, there was not one other soul in that whole cathedral but my friend and me. No one. The light was still there. And when I was finally able to move, I had to be helped up and helped to walk out.

We began wondering where that music came from. There was no sign of a choir, no sign of anything that could have brought in music. But it was music. I was just so glad, so very, very glad to have heard it.

What I realized in Galway was that whatever that mystic experience is, it is share-able. It's possible to talk about it and to have it be understood, even accommodated in other people's experience. But whatever it is—the music of the spheres, resting in the Spirit—it's something that can be passed on. I'm convinced that it can be made real, that it can be something other people would benefit from hearing about.

Interview by James Kimball and Kent Miles
March 4, 1998
Salt Lake City, Utah

Further additions by Emma Lou Thayne
May 2008
Salt Lake City, Utah

Acknowledgements

Many, many people helped to make this book possible. Thank you to those who helped us make contact with the women we interviewed, who made suggestions and comments, offered encouragement and provided help with translation, interpretation, transcription, and editing of the manuscript. To all of you, Jim and I are in your debt.

Joan Kimball and Linda Miles, our wives who were patient, supporting and encouraging throughout the project; Edward Kimball, Cambria Judd, Michelle Williams, Carol Kimball, all of whom provided the needed energy to finish the project; Les Kelen at The Center for Documentary Arts, Elder Hugh Pinnock, Ken and Kate Handley, Reed and Mary Ann Hunter, who helped us contact many of the women in the early stages of interviewing; Francie Wyss, who did the lion's share of transcription; Michael von Rosen, Leni Pilobello, Gabriel Coitiño, Yuri Korolyov, David Robertson, and many other LDS Church Public Affairs officers who helped us connect with these impressive women; Alvina Wall, Tetsuya Tanaka, Diana Peterson, Chad Murphy; Matt Bowen and Daniel Hick for their help in translation.

Many more helped whose names I do not know. Their contributions were no less timely, vital and generous. To all of you, I express my deepest appreciation.